RECLAIMING
HOME

RECLAIMING HOME

DIARY OF A JOURNEY

THROUGH POST-APARTHEID

SOUTH AFRICA

LESEGO MALEPE

SHE WRITES PRESS

Published May 1, 2018
Printed in the United States of America
Print ISBN: 978-1-63152-332-8
E-ISBN: 978-1-63152-333-5
Library of Congress Control Number: 2017961391

For information, address:
She Writes Press
1563 Solano Ave #546
Berkeley, CA 94707

Interior design by Tabitha Lahr

She Writes Press is a division of SparkPoint Studio, LLC.

Names and identifying characteristics have been changed to protect the privacy of certain individuals.

Arnold Howe, Joseph Feroce, Dan Ciccariello,
and Brenda Randolph

PREFACE

When I became a US citizen at the end of 2003, I thought I should celebrate by driving from the East Coast to the West Coast. But it soon occurred to me that I had never traveled through certain important parts of South Africa, my country of origin, since, in the days of apartheid, the many discriminatory laws there made travel for a black person very difficult. It would, I thought, make sense to start there.

In January 2004, therefore, I returned to South Africa, where I crisscrossed the country for myself and in memory of my brother, who had spent twenty-two years on Robben Island, starting in July 1963, when he was eighteen years old.

As I drove, I marveled at my country's beauty and celebrated its ten-year-old freedom while also coming to terms with my past and its past. *Reclaiming Home* is an informative, entertaining, and humorous account of my journey.

TUESDAY, JANUARY 13, 2004.
Hartsfield-Jackson Atlanta International Airport.

I'm sitting in the plane at the airport in Atlanta. The pilot announces that our flight to South Africa will not be a long one. We have the winds in our favor, he says, so we should arrive in Johannesburg ahead of schedule. Nice try! Twelve, thirteen, or fourteen hours . . . it's still a long flight.

WEDNESDAY, JANUARY 14, 2004.
Johannesburg Airport to Mabopane, Pretoria.

We land in Johannesburg ahead of schedule. My friend Lily is late picking me up, which makes me nervous, but before long she arrives. I remember how my father used to be there every time when I arrived for a visit. There was never a time when my plane arrived at the airport before he did. It is hot here—a huge contrast to Boston, where the temperature was in the single digits when I left. This is, of course, because Boston lies in the Northern Hemisphere, where January is wintertime, and Johannesburg lies in the Southern Hemisphere, where January is summertime. I feel lucky and blessed to have the opportunity to escape this year's New England winter.

I sleep all the way to Mabopane, and when Lily wakes me up, we are in front of the gate of my deceased parents' house. I get out of the car to open the gate for my friend, and after her car pulls in, I close it. My eyes are drawn to the rose bush inside the yard and next to the gate. This yellow rose bush my mother loved has buds but no flowers yet—except for one that's almost fully open. Yellow roses were my mother's favorite. I hold it gently and inhale its sweet smell. It's a perfect welcome to my parents' house.

I'm glad to see my younger brother, Kabelo, who lives here and takes care of the house while we work to settle my father's estate.

I sleep well that night, a deep, peaceful sleep in a house that surrounds me with my parents' love, which still lingers there like a sweet, soft scent.

FRIDAY, FEBRUARY 13, 2004.
Pretoria to Pietermaritzburg.

It's Friday the 13th and it's my lucky day, the beginning of my travel across South Africa. This first leg is from Pretoria to Pietermaritzburg, where my cousin Mathabo lives and works. When I call to tell her I'm on my way, she laughs and says she's looking forward to seeing me in the evening when I arrive. When I tell her I'm excited to be hitting the road, she laughs again and says *Matselane.* In Setswana, this is a reference to one who loves the road. Sometimes a girl child who's born while the mother is traveling is named Matselane. She is expected to grow up to love the road.

In the bus, a double-decker, I sit on the lower level, but I don't bother to try to get an empty double-seat by myself because one of the drivers already announced that people should not put their stuff on the seats next to them—that every seat will be filled. I settle down and greet the Indian South African woman next to me, and her warm reply is a good sign of the pleasant journey ahead.

She tells me her name is Anita and she is also going to Pietermaritzburg, where she lives. She is returning from visiting her second son, who invited her to come and stay with his family for a while so she can get out of the depression she's in. I'm surprised but don't mind it when, even before the bus leaves the station in Pretoria, she begins to tell me about her family and her unhappy marriage, the words gushing out like water from a broken pipe.

She sighs deeply and says, "I'm so stressed."

"I'm sorry," I say.

"My husband is seeing another woman," she continues. "A younger woman, and he has a child with her, a young child."

"Oh."

Before I can say anything else, she adds, "Can you believe he told me he was going to bring that woman's child to our house so we will raise it?"

I shake my head in sympathy.

"I won't do it," she says, and I can tell she's trying to convince herself.

She has six children. The one in Pretoria is the son who loves her and has time for her. The others don't seem to care.

I assure her that's usually the case. Children are never the same. There's always one who helps the parents more.

Anita brightens up now as she tells me the details of her children's achievements, and this lasts until we get to Johannesburg—a journey that should have taken forty-five minutes but takes closer to an hour due to heavy traffic. In Johannesburg, we pick up the rest of the passengers who will fill the bus. When we arrive at the station, they load everyone quickly, and as we leave, the driver announces we are now on our way to Durban. We will stop once at a rest stop about halfway there, he says, to give us a chance to stretch and buy things.

Anita comments that the Johannesburg bus station is dilapidated. I agree. After we clear the Johannesburg city area, she continues telling me about her family. Her children have not done too badly, she says, but she wishes they were all like her son, the one who cares about her and recognizes that the husband's behavior is affecting her health. She pauses and looks out the window and seems deep in thought for a while, then she turns to look at me again.

"My husband stresses me so much."

"I'm sorry," I say. "I hope things get better for you at home."

In a softer voice she says, "He stresses me so much, sometimes I'm afraid my head is going to burst and my brain will just be scattered in the street. I always have a headache when I'm home."

This takes me by surprise, and I struggle to come up with the right words to comfort her. "Do you get treatment from your doctor?" I finally ask. "They are good these days about treating all kinds of headaches."

"Thank God my doctor is good! He gives me good medicine for the headaches."

"And," I say, "thank God he's given you a son who cares about you and tries to comfort you and give you a vacation at his house so you can get some relief from the pressure at your home."

"It's so hard the way my husband . . ." She shakes her head, and we are quiet for a while. Then she continues to tell me about her family. She says her son, the second one, has talked to her about selling the house he bought for her and getting her a smaller place. He is tired of supporting everybody, including his younger brother, who still lives with Anita, and his father, who does not contribute to the upkeep of the house.

I can only give her a cliché: "Things will work out at the end."

She smiles and looks at me. "Do you have any children?"

"No."

"Ag shame," she says in a soft voice. It's a common slang phrase that South Africans use when they feel sympathy or pity. Then she asks, "Are you married?"

I smile and say, "Not married."

Again she looks at me with sympathy and softly says, "Ag shame."

I smile and gently say, "I guess everybody is fine the way they are."

She agrees, but I can tell she's not convinced. Better to

have a husband who goes around making babies with other women and expecting to bring them home for the wife to take care of, she believes, than not to have a husband at all. I eschew a serious exploration of the issue with her. All I feel is compassion for this woman who is so stressed. Inside, though, I'm happy that I don't have a husband at this time of my life. Who knows? If I had one, he might have turned out like hers. As for having no children, I don't tell her it's a choice I have never regretted.

Thirty-five minutes after we leave Johannesburg, we've left the urban landscape and the mine dumps just outside the city and entered beautiful farmland. On many of the farms I see the same pattern: a small cluster of little tin houses and a big brick house that is the main house, the farmer's house. We are moving across a land of vast fields of maize, rolling hills and distant valleys filled with shadows in the background. It is green here, no drought like in the north-west part of the country, about which I saw a story in the newspaper the other day. I was shocked by the pictures of all the people at their drought-stricken farms, destitute despite the fact that the government has allocated millions for relief.

The land we are passing through here, though, is lush. We go for miles and miles without seeing towns. There's a little dirt road running parallel to the highway, and I see only a single *bakkie*, small van, driving on it. We also pass a farm where three ostriches stand still near a fence and cows stand unmoving in the field.

My mind is lulled by the humming of the bus on the smooth road and the hypnotic vision of a landscape that, for now, remains unchanging. The driver maintains a steady speed, and after a while it feels as though the bus is moving through the air and not actually touching the ground. I see a big billboard on the side of the road: "AIDS Awareness— Don't be a fool." A few miles down the road, I see another sign: "Grow Tourism." I look up at the clouds. There's a lion in the sky and its mouth, formed by a darker cloud, is slightly open. The play of the lighter and darker clouds makes the cloud picture almost three-dimensional.

Soon we're passing a field of sunflowers. The yellow is muted but intense, as though the flowers are getting ready to explode in the brightest possible yellow and then float upward and brighten the sky.

Windmills dot the landscape, and the long stretches of farmland look quiet, almost lethargic. I can't help but remember the story about a white farmer who, a few days ago, was reported to have thrown a black worker in the lion's den on his farm. The farmer's lion mauled and killed the black worker, leaving only fragments of bones and tattered remnants of his clothes. My mood wants to sink, but I catch it and remind myself that the majority of white farmers are *not* busy feeding black men to their lions.

My thoughts are interrupted by the ringing of a cell phone. The young woman across the aisle answers and begins talking loudly and at length about office politics. Finally she says to the person on the other end of the line, "Your boss is impossible." I wish for the Greyhound buses in my other country, where the drivers announce that phones are to be kept on vibrate and conversations to be kept brief for the comfort of other passengers. The conversation I can't help but overhear is conducted in English with sprinklings of Setswana words here and there, not in Setswana with sprinklings of English words here and there. I'm a bit irritated. Setswana is my language and that's what I speak to those who understand it well in my country. I reflect on language issues and colonialism in South Africa. While accepting that English is the dominant common language, I don't see why people don't speak their own language to each other. Setswana is such a beautiful language.

I've noticed that more young people now speak English even when they don't have to because in some circles it is a status symbol and makes them feel superior showing off their English skills. They are so colonized that they have no love or appreciation for their own languages. I recall instances where newly middle-class black parents proudly announce how their children speak only English. I often ask, "Why can't they speak both?" As children we learned English and Afrikaans at school, but we also learned our home language as well. Things are different now, and middle-class black parents send their children to good, well-resourced former white schools that don't teach African languages, so there is a new generation of African children who do not speak a single African language in their own country. They are few, but I fear their numbers will increase. Colonialism and apartheid may be formally over, but their negative psychological impact remains in some circles.

I smile as I remember the many instances when people commented on how I still spoke my language with them even after living in the United States for many years. They often commented they were glad I had not forgotten my language. I often explained to them that I was in my twenties when I left and there was no way I could forget to speak my language. Some would make fun of people who after being overseas for a few months would come back pretentious and speak English with a new nasal twang and pretend to struggle with their own languages. They often laughed and made fun of such people.

One of the main things I look forward to when visiting my country is that I will be able to speak my language or another indigenous language almost exclusively. I also remember how I looked forward to speaking to my father on the phone when he was alive and speaking Setswana. He spent most of his professional life teaching, translating, and doing research on Setswana at the University of South Africa and instilled in us, his children, a love of Setswana, so much that in college I was torn between pursuing a teaching career in political science and pursuing one in Setswana. The highest grade I ever got in college was in Setswana as a subject. I catch myself and remind myself that I'm celebrating my country's democracy and I should not dwell on irritating subjects so early in the trip. This poor young woman is growing up in circumstances where the formerly colonized feel inferior and see everything white as more valuable and do not appreciate their culture and traditions. Apartheid and colonialism may be over, but the psychological damage is still around. I soften and feel kind toward this young woman and look in her direction and smile. I notice she is now speaking Setswana with sprinklings of some English words and I am pleased. My mood is upbeat again and I enjoy the passing landscape.

Another sign on the side of the road implores drivers to "Stay Alive, Stay Alert." Almost everyone around me is asleep or at least has their eyes closed. Another sign says, "Tourism Creates Jobs." What kind, I wonder, and for whom? I think of a recent case where a young European woman was killed by a white man who robbed her after she gave him a ride. Crime is a big problem in South Africa, and tourists often forget that there are white criminals here. It's hard to blame them, of course, because to hear many people who live here talk about crime, it is a simple matter of white victims and black criminals.

As we enter the Montrose area, I see the dramatic mountain peaks on the left. They become more and more spectacular as we drive farther into the area. One looks like a miniature Table Mountain.

The bus driver announces that the bus will stop at a rest stop for twenty-five minutes and everyone should feel free to get out and get refreshments and food. Outside, I walk around and stretch my legs. Mountains surround us. I wonder what it must feel like to see this view every day.

From Montrose onward, the view is the unrelieved beauty of hills and valleys and little dirt roads and paths meandering around the hills. Gorges crisscross the landscape, and here and there are *dongas*, little houses, that reinforce the simple beauty of this land. It is intensely green all over. Here, the drought is another country. Cattle laze around in the tender, soft light the sun is struggling to send out from behind the clouds. Dancing shadows form interesting patterns on the ground: deep shadows in the valleys, the short shadows of trees, and the long shadows cast on the sides of the hills. The hills, peaks, and huge standing rocks all have different shapes, as though carved by an artist.

Rain starts falling and darkness descends. It is soothing.

Finally we reach Pietermaritzburg, the last stop before Durban and the city where Gandhi once lived. I bid Anita good-bye and wish her the best. She wishes me a good time in Pietermaritzburg. My cousin Mathabo picks me up, and we go to her home.

Mathabo and I stay up late catching up. When I finally go to bed, I sleep well.

SATURDAY, FEBRUARY 14, 2004.
Pietermaritzburg.

Mathabo and I decide not to do anything special today. We take a long walk to the supermarket, then come back to her house, sit on the enclosed porch, and talk about her job at the area's Land Commission Office. I feel fortunate to have my dear cousin working for the Department of Land Affairs because I am interested in the land issue and how it is being handled by the department.

"It must feel good being involved in this historical meaningful work," I say.

"It sure does," Mathabo says. "My office is settling many land claims and the government is compensating people whose lands were taken by the apartheid government."

"I know it is not much given what people have gone through," I say, "but it is a good gesture, to help wipe away the tears."

"It is not much," Mathabo says. "But at least it is something—it is a public acknowledgement of the injustice they went through." She pauses. "I wanted to tell you in person: our land claim for the forced removal from our parents' house in Brakpan has just been settled."

"That's great," I say. "It is wonderful." I remember fondly how I used to visit that home in Brakpan, near Johannesburg, and think of her parents, who have since died.

"We have just received compensation for our parents' house," Mathabo says. "The five of us will share the money awarded—fifty thousand rands."

Given the exchange rate, that comes to about US$20,000.

"We are also about to have our old Kilnerton land claim approved," I tell her. "We should be getting a settlement in the next four months."

"I assume you will be getting a settlement not only for your parents' house but for your grandmother's house and fruit farm as well," Mathabo says.

"Yes, and remember, Koko"—that's my grandmother—"owned the store in the village too," I say. "I'm not sure how those differences will be handled."

We are quiet for a while.

"Koko really lost a lot," I finally say. "She was never the same again, and she never went into business again."

"It's a shame they are not here to see their loss acknowledged," Mathabo says. "With at least some token compensation."

I nod. "That is sad, that most of them died before this."

We fall silent again.

In 1954, my parents, together with other Kilnerton residents, were forcibly removed from their land in Pretoria because the government wanted it for white people. My maternal grandmother also lost her house, neighborhood store, and farm in the forced removal—all this without compensation. Even the graves, including my grandfather's, were dug up. Up to the end, my grandmother grieved for her property and the loss of income she used to generate from the old Kilnerton farm and corner store. Many people, including my brothers, were radicalized by these forced removals.

I sense that we are about to get depressed, so I quickly decide to change the subject, but Mathabo beats me to it.

"Did you see the story in the newspapers about the white farmer who fed a black worker to the lions?" she asks.

I shudder. "Yes, I saw it."

She shakes her head. "Unbelievable."

"Even with a black government, racism and the idea of white entitlement are so ingrained, especially in the rural areas, that some white farmers continue to act like nothing has changed," I say.

She frowns. "Old habits die hard. While there may be change on the surface, deep down, a lot of people are the same."

"Change is slow," I say. "It is comforting that there is a difference though—this time there are consequences. That farmer will be charged and go to jail. In the olden days he would have gotten away with murder."

"Human beings don't change easily," she says.

"So many white people used to murder black people and not go to jail," I say. "At least now all lives are equal under the law."

"It will take time but hearts will change," she says. "I hope."

"The next generation," I say. "Maybe there is hope."

"Remember I told you about my friend who is a white woman I usually hike with?" she asks.

"Yes, the one you go to yoga with sometimes?"

Mathabo nods. "One day she told me how her father hates blacks. She said his attitude pained her."

"I feel for her," I say. "It is encouraging that someone who grew up in such a hateful home turned out not to be evil. What did you say?"

"I tried to make her feel better by saying her father was part of a generation where that is not unusual, and that we cannot be responsible for other people's beliefs, not even our parents'."

"This should make us appreciate our parents," I say. "They worked so hard to help us avoid hating whites."

SUNDAY, FEBRUARY 15, 2004.
Pietermaritzburg.

Mathabo and I have been invited to dinner by Liz, one of her Indian friends. Mathabo says when she told her that her cousin was visiting from Pretoria, Liz said, "Please bring her over for dinner midday on Sunday. You're such a lovely person, I would like to meet someone who's part of your family." My cousin says she laughed at that and told Liz that I happened to be nice, but not everybody in our family is nice. We have our own problems, just like every family.

When we arrive at Liz's house, she's happy to see us and introduces us to her daughter and grandchild. We settle on the porch and her daughter immediately serves us fresh, homemade granadilla juice. It is such a treat. Ripe granadillas have an ugly, wrinkled, purple-brownish skin.

"They're trying to hide the beauty inside so we are pleasantly surprised by their sweet juice once we crack them open and drink," I say.

Mathabo and Liz look at each other and smile, and Liz says, "You're right 'Thabi. She has a way with words." Then Liz turns to me and says, "Your cousin told me I would enjoy your company, that you were a joy to be with because you express yourself so musically."

"That's not true," I protest.

Mathabo says nothing, but she has a big smile on her face.

In a mock scolding, I say, "Liz, don't believe everything

she says. It's just that she loves me and she says these wonderful but untrue good things about me."

"I believe her." Liz smiles. "I won't tell you the other nice things she said about you which I know to be true. I don't want you to be embarrassed."

The two laugh. I scowl at Mathabo.

"Now, let's talk about important things," I say. Liz starts to say something, but I chime in quickly, "You know something, Liz?"

"Yes?" she says. She and Mathabo look at each other and then at me.

"Granadillas are among the little things that we dream about when we are living far away in America." I rub my fingers together. "The texture"—I close my eyes, sniff the air—"the smell, heavenly."

Liz smiles. "As long as you are in Pietermaritzburg, I'll make sure you have sweet granadilla juice to drink."

I grin. "Thank you so much, Liz."

"You see," Mathabo says, "I told you, she'll do anything to stop me from telling you good things about her."

"I love granadillas," I say, refusing to engage on that topic.

I'm relieved when at this point, Liz's daughter calls us in for dinner. On the table are nine dishes: a chicken curry, a lamb biryani, lentils in a mild tomato sauce, cabbage, squash, baked chicken (in case I don't like the flavor of the spices in the curry), string beans, beetroot in a mild vinaigrette dressing, and rice.

"This is a feast!" I exclaim.

"It's just a Sunday meal," Liz says. "I'd like to cook you a real feast one day."

"I'm tempted to sink roots here if this is what I can have, even if it is only once a year. This is a feast."

As we begin to eat, Liz says, "Mathabo has been a good friend and often gives me a ride when she goes to her home in Brakpan at the end of the month. I have a daughter near Jo'burg, so I appreciate being able to visit her so easily. It wouldn't be possible to go so frequently if it were not for Mathabo."

"This is nothing, really, because I'm going to my own home and it's nice to have company," Mathabo says.

"Yes," I say. "Mathabo is the best travel companion in the world."

I'm amused as they go on back and forth, one saying it's a great help and the other downplaying her good deeds as nothing.

After dinner, Liz's daughter clears the table and I thank her.

"It's nothing," she says.

I attempt to get up from the table, but Liz says, "Don't run away, there's dessert coming."

"Did Mathabo tell you I love desserts?" I say. "But please give us at least an hour's rest before dessert."

Mathabo rubs her tummy and protests, "We are going to burst."

We laugh.

Liz looks at Mathabo. "But it's your favorite trifle. We can't wait too long because at four o'clock we have to have tea with special biscuits."

Biscuits too? My stomach hurts just thinking about eating more.

We retire to the living room, where we relax for a while before having the trifle and tea around three. Liz allows us to skip the cookies.

I take my first bite of trifle and sigh with pleasure. "This is a perfect day. And this is the best trifle, Liz. I thank you for your generosity."

She laughs. "It's nothing. This is how we live. When a friend's family visits, we do this."

I sense that this may be a jab at America, but I'm not about to spoil our languid afternoon with explanations or a defense of my adopted country.

When we leave, I thank Liz again and promise to come back one day.

"Mathabo, show her where I work," Liz says. "That way she can come and spend her days there with me while you are at work. At my place she can read or write or do anything because she won't be disturbing anything. And she can see all kinds of interesting people."

"Thank you, I'd like that," I say.

Mathabo looks at me. "You will like it. The market is right next to our office building."

"Come tomorrow," Liz says. "Interesting people come and go. I'll fill you in on the gossip. It is nice to work for oneself."

"Yes," I say. "I won't be in the way. I'll bring a book."

"Don't worry," she says, "I can sew and talk at the same time."

I feel lucky.

When we arrive at the house of another of Mathabo's friends, a woman named Niki, she greets us warmly. "Lesego," she says, "I've wanted to meet you for so long. Mathabo talks about you and misses you."

"I miss her so much too," I say. "Niki, thank you so much for inviting us."

She laughs. "Mathabo, you can tell she's lived in America for too long. What's this thank-you for inviting you?" She turns to me and adds, "Mathabo and I are friends and you're a cousin—no, more like a sister—so you're part of the circle here. We are sister-friends and we visit all the time here."

I laugh too. "Sorry for sounding so formal. Forgive me. Having had to start life from scratch in a foreign country, I don't take such kindness and generosity for granted. I've lived long enough to know that I'm lucky."

The two of them laugh and Niki says, "I'm Mathabo's closest friend here so you're sister-friend and family too, no formalities."

"Thanks," I say. "I appreciate it."

"No, no, no formalities, my sister," Niki says.

"Yes," I say to Niki. "But just so you know, living in the US this long does not mean I've forgotten certain things. You're young, much younger than me, so I have many years over you."

She laughs at that and claps her hands. "I should be forgiven my impudence, dear sister. I apologize."

We all laugh out loud.

"Lesego is smart," Mathabo says. "She was in a corner and she pulled age rank, knowing that being so well brought up you couldn't go on making fun of her formal European ways."

"I know I'm home," I say. "It's nice to be in a place where age can get me some advantages."

"My sister, I admit age is important, though I respectfully submit that, fortunately, the age difference is not too great," Niki says. "Otherwise I'd be fined a whole cow."

Now it's my turn again. "What? Now you're all modern and a few years don't matter anymore? I don't know how old you think I am. I may be a few years younger than Mathabo, but I'm much older than you, young lady."

She claps her hands together again. "*Uxolo Sisi*," she says, asking for forgiveness. She understands the scolding is playful.

This is banter that can only take place between two people who understand each other's cultures very well. I'm glad to be here.

We all sit in front of the garage. The garage door is open, and I see the carcass of a sheep hanging in the garage. "What's the occasion?" I nod toward the sheep.

"My boss's assignment," Niki says.

Her boss is the project manager for her team at the Land Affairs Department. Mathabo is also a project manager but leads a different team.

"I like this assignment as long as the meat stays here," I say.

"Two days ago," Niki says, "our team in the department went to a village about two hundred miles away to hand land back to a group that has won the right to it after having it confiscated by force and without compensation by the previous government. This was a big land claim settlement, so the minister of Land Affairs did the handing over. It was a big event, and the community prepared a big feast for everybody. They thanked the project manager, my boss, with the sheep and the minister with a cow."

"Both were walking," I say. "Was the sheep alive when you brought it here?"

"Yes," Niki says. "Friends of mine came earlier in the day and slaughtered and cleaned it. My boss said to take half of the sheep and her son will pick up the other half."

"Good boss," I say.

"We are going to cook some of it on an open fire so we can eat."

"Today is a day of eating," I say.

"Yes, we celebrate with the poor people who got their land back," Mathabo says.

"Lucky for them," Niki says, "their lands were kept as farms. So they chose to take the land back."

"The farmers were compensated," Mathabo says.

As we talk about farms, I'm reminded of the beautiful flowers I saw when we drove in. "I'm going to the front of the house to look at your lovely flowers," I say. "I like how colorful they are."

"Mathabo told me you would immediately notice the beauty," Niki says.

I nod. "Flowers are what I miss in Boston, where I don't have a garden—which is just as well, given how short the growing season in Massachusetts is."

"It's a pity she is not here for very long," Mathabo tells Niki as they follow me to the front of the house. "She would help you with the garden."

I quickly add, "Yes, I'd take care of the flowers, but at the back I'd plant some spinach and beans and tomatoes and some herbs."

Niki nudges my cousin. "Mathabo, we should persuade her to come back to live in South Africa."

I just smile and survey the building in front of me. "I like the old brick houses like yours, Niki. They are beautiful and solid."

"Sisi, these houses in this area, you see they look alike, were government-subsidized and owned houses for white South African Railways workers." She shrugs.

I shake my head. "Even uneducated whites had it good. Their lives were so heavily subsidized."

"With the new democracy, however, these government-owned and subsidized houses were sold and white railway workers had to rent or buy them like everybody else," Mathabo says.

I shake my head. "It is amazing how even for this class of railway workers, who were not educated or highly skilled, the previous government built beautiful houses with garages and maids' quarters. Yes, folks, apartheid was a good ride for white people."

Niki nods. "Ja, it was really something."

"The 'my vel is my MA' brigade must be disoriented because they are unskilled white people and there is no white government to provide white welfare," I say.

Niki and Mathabo laugh.

"Those days are over," Niki says.

"My vel is my MA" is an Afrikaans saying that in English means, "My skin is my MA degree." That is what working-class drunk white men used to say when they came up against a well-dressed and obviously educated, middle-class black man.

"The yellow roses are beautiful, Niki," I say. "They were my mother's favorite. You have to come and visit us in Pretoria. When you step through the gate, you will be greeted by big yellow roses."

"'Sego's mother loved flowers and her big garden was beautiful," Mathabo tells her. "At the back she planted vegetables, which always thrived, and we ate spinach straight from the garden and it had a sweetness to it."

"And she worked on it herself and she was a schoolteacher," I say. "I don't know how she did it."

"The city council ran garden competitions in Mamelodi and for many, many years the results were predictable," Mathabo continues. "A man a few blocks away won first prize, Lesego's mother's brother won second prize, and Lesego's mother won third prize."

"Ooh, ooh," Niki exclaimed and clapped her hands.

"Here's something else," I said. "The man who won first prize did not work and the garden was his full-time job. He was an herbalist who lived a simple life and saw a few clients at night, and his garden was big because his house was small, whereas my mother's garden was much smaller because the extended bigger house took more space that would have been used by the garden. My uncle who took second place had two stands and a huge garden and had two boys who helped him after school."

"Her mother's garden was prettier," Mathabo says.

"My mother and uncle got their love of gardening from their parents. They say my grandfather loved planting flowers. By the way, my grandmother had a large fruit farm in

Pretoria, which the government took away. That farm used to supply vegetables and fruit to the Kilnerton boarding school. Whites did not want any competition from black farmers." I sigh. "Anyway, let's not think about those things today. Let's celebrate."

"I'm glad my work helps to expose all that evil of apartheid," Mathabo says.

We admire the red roses. I cut one and place it in my braids and Niki adjusts it. "Looks so nice on you," she says with an approving smile.

The garden is brimming with color. I smell the yellow carnations and admire small white flowers I had not seen before. Then I ask Niki about the racial makeup of this suburb, which I've been curious about since we got here.

"It is mixed, but the new black homeowners are middle-class, whereas the remaining whites are working-class," she says.

When Niki's son comes to tell us the grill is ready, we retire to the back of the house.

Niki puts big slabs of mutton on. Mathabo and I sit in the shade on benches in front of the garage and watch as Niki, with the help of her daughter, tends to the meat.

"I'm glad I'm going to have fresh mutton, not the kind that has been refrigerated for a long time," I say.

"In this area we usually get fresh meat," Mathabo says.

I notice there is a lot going on in the kitchen. "I see from that activity we are going to have a big dinner. Yum."

"Yes, Sisi, the girls are making you some treats," Niki calls from her position at the grill.

"I'm going to hug these kids," I say.

One of the boys places a low table in front of us.

"Or would you prefer to go eat inside?" Niki asks.

"The light this time of day is soft and a light, delicate orange," I say. "And the sky is a calm, end-of-the-day blue. This is heaven. Let's eat outside."

"Remember it is cold in Boston," Mathabo says, raising an eyebrow.

She and Niki laugh.

"We are lucky," I say. "Look at the streaks of light orange sunlight between the tree branches."

The two laugh again.

"Sisi," Niki says, "You have to come here every year."

One of the young girls comes with a bowl of warm water and soap, a pink towel draped over her shoulder. I wash my hands, then take towel from her shoulder and dry my hands. After I thank her, she goes to Mathabo and to Niki. Another girl places special wooden bowls common to the area on the low table in front of us.

"Thank you, this looks beautiful," I say.

"No waiting, Sisi," Niki says. "Let's celebrate."

I look at Mathabo and she says, "Go ahead, 'Sego, we eat the meat by itself first. It is like an appetizer."

"We eat this in front of us first, and then when we're done, they'll bring us more meat and *jeqa*," Niki says, gesturing toward the food.

I reach for one of the bowls.

The sun has set now and the air is a bit cooler. We continue to sit outside and eat meat and *jeqa,* the steamed bread common in the area.

"Thank you, Niki," I say. "This meat is so tender and this *jeqa* is the best I've ever had."

"Yes, Niki makes the best *jeqa*!" Mathabo agrees.

Niki waves a hand as if to dismiss our praise. "It is so easy," she says.

It is after eight o'clock when we say our good-byes and thank Niki for a perfect day. On the way to Mathabo's house, I tell her she's lucky to have friends like these.

I read today's *City Press* when we get back to Mathabo's, and there is an article about the arrest of a former security policeman named Gideon Niewoudt in connection with the 1985 murders of the Pebco Three, who were anti-apartheid activists. Niewoudt admitted in the Truth and Reconciliation Commission (TRC) hearing that he took part in the murders, and the TRC refused to grant him amnesty because it determined he had not disclosed the full extent of his crimes, a condition for the granting of amnesty and protection from prosecution by the TRC. Niewoudt appeared in court in Port Elizabeth and was granted bail of R50,000. He is scheduled to go on trial in June. The article quoted the mother of Godolozi, one of the murdered activists, as saying, "I am happy that the man who is behind the death of my son and his friends is at last taken to court."

I say a silent prayer, thanking God for saving my brother Dimake, who survived extreme torture in 1963 and a life sentence on Robben Island and lived to see the death of apartheid.

In the same paper, an editorial declares, "The arrest of former Eastern Cape security policeman Gideon Niewoudt in connection with the 1985 murders of the Eastern Cape anti-apartheid activists who became known as the Pebco Three is surely good news for the families of those who died at the hands of the apartheid security forces.

"Niewoudt's arrest will make shivers run down the

spines of those who stubbornly refused to embrace the spirit of reconciliation so generously offered to them by the Truth and Reconciliation Commission."

The author of the editorial concludes the piece by saying, "It is undoubtedly this same racist mentality that drove a white Limpopo employer to allegedly feed one of his ex-workers to a lion. We hope that justice will, in both cases, take its course and be seen to be done."

I have a hard time falling asleep tonight, caught up in reliving the events of 1963 and their impact on my family. I remember our fear that the security police were going to kill my brother. I remember how in sentencing the judge said he would have imposed the death penalty if Dimake were not so young, eighteen years old. I was thirteen years old at the time, and the joy and innocence of my childhood died that day.

MONDAY, FEBRUARY 16, 2004.
Pietermaritzburg.

A young woman directs me to an Internet café in Pieter-maritzburg, a couple of blocks away. I don't mind the walk since this city is a walking city. On my way there, I pass a slim white woman wearing high heels, a short skirt, and a tight-fitting shirt. I look again and realize it's a man. After he goes by, I look back again and see that he's swaying his narrow hips in an exaggerated rhythm.

At the next block I stop at the statue of Mahatma Gandhi, the Indian lawyer who fought for the rights of Indians in South Africa—people who, like black people, were discriminated against and suffered daily humiliations over the course of this country's history.

At the Internet café, I check my email and respond to a few friends. Next I go to visit Liz, Mathabo's Indian friend, at her place of work, which is a stall in an enclosed, city-sponsored market of little stalls used by shoemakers, seamstresses, and other small businesses.

Liz tells me she's been looking forward to my visit—business is slow this time of year. But our conversation is interrupted when a smiling young black woman holding a pad and pen comes in.

Liz frowns. "Back again? What do they want this time?"

"No, ma'am," the young woman says apologetically, "it's just a small survey, so the city can improve things for business."

Liz is not impressed. "Improve things?" She looks at me and says, "All they want to do is increase our rents. That's all they want to do."

Still smiling, the young woman says, "No, ma'am, honestly, it is to see how they can improve things so they can help you improve your businesses so you can make more money." She puts pen to paper. "Please, just a few questions to answer."

Liz isn't ready to comply yet. "How come I didn't see you go into the other stalls?"

The smiling woman explains she's interviewing all stall occupants. She asks a few questions and thanks Liz.

As the young woman exits the stall, Liz says in a loud voice, "Everybody is after Indians."

The young woman looks back and smiles again. I can tell she's used to this, and I'm glad she sees humor in it. I also feel sympathy for Liz. Such general insecurity about the new dispensation, normal in all political transitions, has to be difficult.

That evening, when I tell Mathabo about the man dressed in the high heels and tight shirt, she laughs and says he's harmless and everybody knows him. I tell her no one gave him a second look. Then I tell my cousin about Liz saying, "Everybody is after Indians." I add that I was tempted to probe, but decided to meet her several more times before I ask such a loaded question. I want Liz to be more comfortable with me and trust me. Mathabo replies that Liz is very open and would probably be happy to have someone listen to her with sympathy regarding what she perceives as the disadvantageous position of Indians. It is easy to feel marginalized as a minority.

I wish I'd known Liz during apartheid so I could find out if her views have changed or if she's always thought everybody is "after" Indians. Mathabo agrees that would be interesting, and laments that that is one of the tragedies of apartheid: it kept the races strictly separated and made social relations across the color line very difficult. I consider myself fortunate to be living the life of an academic in the United States; it is a life that naturally helps me interact meaningfully with people of different heritages and from various parts of the world.

TUESDAY, FEBRUARY 17, 2004.
Pietermaritzburg.

In the afternoon, when I go to town again and ask a young woman for directions to Victoria Mall, instead of merely giving me directions, she walks three blocks with me. On the way, we talk about how different things are now. She is hoping to go to nursing school next year. I wish her luck. She bids me good-bye at the entrance of the mall and goes back the way we came. I later regret not treating her to a meal or at least a coffee.

When I meet Mathabo, we drive to a fish and chips shop at the small mall near her house. We order fish and chips to take home.

"It's very good," she assures me.

"I hope so," I say.

"Do you think this will match your childhood memory of Spartan's fish and chips?" she asks.

I laugh as I recall the day in Springs, a town on the East Rand, when I complained that the fish and chips was not as good as the ones we'd had when we were children at Spartan's. Mathabo said that day that nothing could ever compete with that memory because a lot of pleasant things went with it. That's when I realized that there would never be fish and chips to compete with the Spartan's fish and chips of my childhood.

Mathabo next tells me she had a nice call from the white friend she often hikes with—the one who told her that her father is racist and hates black people. She is on vacation and says she regrets she will not return in time to meet me before I leave Pietermaritzburg. I say there'll be a next time.

As we park Mathabo's car, she tells me about one of her white neighbors at the apartment complex. The wife and kids greet her cordially, but the man frowns when he sees Mathabo, who is the only black person in that complex.

"It must be very difficult for the white man because he's working-class and never went to college, and here is the only black person in his complex and she is better educated and has a senior position in the government," I say. "He's been lied to all his life, and I feel sorry for him."

WEDNESDAY, FEBRUARY 18, 2004.
Pietermaritzburg.

Today I walk in town for two hours and then stop by Liz's stall again, as I promised her I would. I am eager to talk with her and learn how she sees herself in her community and in the larger society.

Liz is happy to see me and says she has been looking forward to my visit and hopes I've brought my books with me so I can stay the whole day. "I've been looking forward to hanging out with you," I tell her.

"Business is slow and I'm lonely," she says. "I'm grateful for your company!"

"I appreciate your company, too," I say, "and I wish there was a way I could help in your business."

Not too long after I sit down with Liz, a young African woman walks in. She, too, is very polite and, just like with yesterday's city council employee, smiles too much. This makes Liz irritated and suspicious. When the young woman hands Liz some registration forms, Liz says she does not understand why Indians like her have to register. She keeps her arms folded. The young woman lays the forms on the table and says they just want to "straighten their records."

"Nobody is going to charge or tax you," she assures Liz.

I gather that these stalls are subsidized by the city, and the small traders who use them live in fear of one day being charged rent.

I'm fascinated by Liz's view of authority and wish I could talk to the city council employee and learn about the building and the city's plans for it. But I restrain myself; I do not wish to do anything that would irritate Liz and make her trust me less. The fact that the city employee is African complicates things. It would be easier if she was Indian because then it would not look like I was ganging up with her against Liz and other Indians.

After the young city employee leaves, Liz frowns and says, "They're always . . . everybody always goes after Indians, even traffic police go to Indian areas and target Indian drivers."

I ask her if these are Zulu traffic police. I deliberately say Zulu rather than African so I can distance myself a little. Liz knows I'm not Zulu and do not come from this area. I'm hoping she might elaborate and speak frankly about her fears as a minority, as she's speaking to someone who is not from this area. But she does not seem interested in elaborating. She just says, "Everybody."

We are quiet for a while. I break the silence and the somber mood by pointing out that the picture of Halle Berry on the wall is beautiful.

"I like it a lot," Liz says. "Halle Berry is very beautiful."

"Yes," I agree. "She's one of my favorite actors."

Liz tilts her head a bit and smiles. "Mixed is more beautiful, sometimes more beautiful than white."

"Are whites your standard for beauty?" I ask her gently.

She's a bit startled and considers this for a minute. Then, in a dismissive tone, she says, "They're just white."

Mathabo joins us a bit later, and Liz tells her she is enjoying my company and Mathabo should not take me away. But we have to leave, so I promise to stop by again soon.

As Mathabo and I go to do her errands, I tell her how Liz complained again about "everybody being after Indians." I knew there was a lot of anxiety in all sectors of the society when the government changed, but this is normal during transitions when societies are trying to carve a new path. Even whites, who still own the bulk of the wealth of the country, feel anxious and oppressed sometimes.

My cousin agrees that much in life these days is uncertain. "We are all learning to navigate the new South Africa," she says, "and it is not easy." She's silent for a moment, then adds, "I've heard that Coloureds often say that during apartheid, when whites ruled, they were not white enough and now that blacks are ruling, they are not black enough."

Mathabo now tells me that not too long ago two traffic police, one Coloured (mixed ethnic origin) and one Indian, stopped her. It was clear the Indian hoped for a bribe from her, but she was determined not to bribe him, so he gave her a ticket.

"It is cheaper to give a little bribe," she says, "but I am determined not to bribe any traffic police." She shakes her head. "I was so angry."

"Were you mad because he was Indian?" I ask.

She laughs. "I've thought a lot about why I felt so angry that day. But I've had encounters with other traffic police, not Indians, and have often gotten just as angry." She purses her lips. "I've told myself I will never bribe to avoid a ticket, no matter how expensive. Bribery encourages corruption."

Now it's my turn. I tell Mathabo about how angry I got one day while I was traveling with a friend in a township in Pretoria and we were stopped by two black traffic cops, one of whom came to the driver's window and said that one of the tires on my friend's car was "smooth." I could tell my friend was used to being stopped like that because he was driving an old car. He tried to plead for mercy, arguing respectfully (and correctly) that the tire was only borderline smooth. They argued back and forth, and my friend pled with the African cop to be lenient. The officer finally asked him to come outside so they could solve it in "the people's way." My friend got out of the car, and they went to the back of the car and continued bargaining. My friend was happy when he got back in the car and drove away—he felt they had arrived at a satisfactory settlement. But I was seething inside, especially because the traffic cop was black. I had hoped for better after our hard-won struggle. However, I was not really surprised. I remember how in the past black taxi drivers used to joke that they always budgeted for bribes to give to white traffic officers.

After hearing my story, Mathabo goes back to her office, and I walk to Victoria Mall, where I go into an Internet café and check my email. Later I buy newspapers and go into a café and drink tea and read. There's a story about a maid who was raped by her employer.

THURSDAY, FEBRUARY 19, 2004.
Pietermaritzburg.

I think about the previous day's events and write to clarify my thoughts. South Africa has special traffic police who are not regular police officers. They have always been considered corrupt. A short while before I left the country in 1978, I was stopped by a black traffic cop at an intersection with a four-way stop. He said I did not make a full stop. I said I thought I had made a full stop. He gave a long explanation about how to make a full stop, as though it was complicated. I looked at him and smiled and said I appreciated the explanation. He said the car was a nice car and I thanked him for the compliment and said it should be directed at my father. "He has a good child," I said. "I try very hard to be moral." I could tell he was hoping to get a small bribe. He did not get it. I got a ticket. I thanked him politely and left. I remember feeling triumphant for having denied him a bribe.

Thinking about Liz's remarks now and what she said about traffic cops targeting Indians, I feel sad and sorry for her. I resolve to discuss the issue further with her and to somehow find a way to make her feel better. I plan to tell her that most traffic cops—of all colors—are corrupt. It is the culture of the traffic police force as a whole that is corrupt, and they target everybody. I also reflect on how South Africa is in a transition after a horrible history and how this creates all kinds of insecurity, especially for minorities. It is understandable that South African Coloureds and Indians would feel insecure, given their small numbers and the fact that during apartheid they suffered a lot at the hands of the white government but in some respects may have been considered more privileged by the African majority. For example, the apartheid government spent much more by far on the education of Coloureds and Indians than on the education of Africans (as blacks were called in the past). They did not have the full privileges of white people, but they did not have all the disadvantages of being African. Divide and rule was a deliberate strategy that at the end was not completely successful, since many Indians and Coloureds fought in the liberation struggle alongside the majority.

I understand Liz's anxiety and resolve to discuss these issues with her in a way I hope will make her feel better.

South Africa has a long way to go, but at least we are now trying to build a better society.

FRIDAY, FEBRUARY 20, 2004.
Pietermaritzburg.

The sun is up and it's bright early. The sky is a light, soothing blue, the blue of the ocean on a sunny, clear day. As we get into the car, I say to Mathabo, "The sky is just wonderful today. This kind of blue makes me feel like I'm floating." We've been through my weather comments many times, but I can't resist here in South Africa. It's beautiful like this most of the time. I cannot say the same for my beloved Boston.

Mathabo drops me off at the Internet café, where I check my email. All my arrangements for my Baz Bus trip to Durban and beyond are confirmed. (Baz Bus advertises itself as a "backpacker's" bus. You "jump on and jump off.") Next I email the youth hostel where I'll be staying on Sunday night. The quality of youth hostels is very uneven, and I don't know much about the place. But I'm not worried. I'll be there for only one night, and the following morning I'll continue with the Baz Bus to Port Elizabeth in the Eastern Cape Province, where Mandela grew up and now has a house.

Done with checking my email at the internet café, I walk to the library.

At the entrance to the library, I see a notice that reads, "Voluntary Workers—We regret that we are no longer able to accept voluntary workers in any department or branch of this library." Unemployment is high, and the newspaper area in the library is crowded with young people looking at job advertisements. In the *Mail & Guardian*, the leading weekly, there's a story about suicides and trains in Botswana. Tebelelo Seretse, Botswana's Minister of Works and Transport, is quoted on page 41 as saying, "I am appealing to the people not to use the trains to kill themselves. If people want to commit suicide they should use trees, not our trains."

SATURDAY, FEBRUARY 21, 2004.
Pietermaritzburg.

Mathabo and I enjoy a stroll through Pietermaritzburg's Botanical Gardens on this warm but cloudy summer day, then go to a coffee shop at the Midlands Mall nearby, where we sit by a window and watch the rain pound the glass. Flashes of lightning crisscross the sky, and suddenly the lights go off. Before long, thank goodness, emergency lights come on.

I remind Mathabo of how when we were children we thought the Ndebele people could harness lightning and use it to hurt those who had wronged them. When we were children, Ndebele women used to come from nearby farms carrying bundles of sugarcane on their heads to sell in Mamelodi township. There was an often-repeated story about how one day, one of them put her bundle down so a woman could choose a cane to buy. A big boy tried to take one of the canes without paying, and the Ndebele woman just looked at him without fear and said, "*Ngizo ku ratha nge Tladi*," meaning she would strike the boy with lightning if he robbed her. It stopped him cold; he walked away. A lot of people, petty thieves included, believed the Ndebele had this power, which was good for them; it protected them from being robbed as they sold their wares in the township.

Today there's a story in one of the local papers about the hijacking of an ambulance by the men who called for it. When it got there, they forced the two attendants, a man and a woman, to turn over the vehicle, and then they raped the woman in front of the man. When he pleaded with them not to hurt her, they beat him up. Ambulances now have to be accompanied by the police when they respond to calls.

SUNDAY, FEBRUARY 22, 2004.
Pietermaritzburg to Durban.

I get up early and go out to buy newspapers at a convenience store around the corner. The Sunday *Times* has a story about language problems at the University of Stellenbosch, the intellectual cradle of apartheid from which most South African prime ministers and presidents graduated. Black students are protesting and complaining that they don't understand lectures delivered in Afrikaans.

As much as I'm enjoying my time with my cousin, I am also looking forward to hitting the road again. In the afternoon, Mathabo takes me to the Ngena Youth Hostel, where we wait for the Baz Bus to Durban. I go in to see the inside of the hostel. It is utilitarian and plain, but very clean. I hope the one I'm going to spend the night at in Durban will be as good!

The fifteen-seater Baz Bus arrives, and I'm glad to be on my way. The young Indian driver speaks to his black codriver in perfect Zulu, and the drive to Durban is pleasant; the snaking roads hypnotize me into a meditative state. My mind seems to go up and down with the green hills of this area.

When we arrive in Durban, where all passengers will spend the night, we stop in front of the youth hostel. As soon as I see it, I'm alarmed by how rundown the place looks, but I quickly remind myself not to judge a book by its cover. It may surprise me with beauty inside.

The driver helps me carry my bags into the hostel, and I ask him to wait until I've registered to make sure there's room. I tell him that when I called to reserve a room, the man who answered the phone declined to take my name. All he said was, "There's room," and my email got no reply.

The young black man at the desk is not rude, but he's indifferent as he asks my name and I tell him. I add that the person who took my call said it was not necessary to take my name. When the desk clerk says there's a double room, the Baz Bus driver tells me he'll pick me up in the morning to continue the journey to Port Elizabeth. But he can see I'm worried, so he leans over and whispers in my ear, "You'll be fine and safe. Don't worry, tomorrow you're going to enjoy the drive to PE."

I wonder if I should go to the Holiday Inn I know is three blocks away. It would be more expensive, I realize, but it might be worth it. I whisper back to the driver, "Baz Bus should have told me this place is a dump. Baz Bus should not have it on its list of youth hostel stops."

He merely smiles and says, "We'll talk tomorrow."

I look around. The walls in the small lobby are dark green and there's no shine on them. The desk clerk carries my heavy bag up the old wooden stairs, which creak and croak and protest every single step. I try to step more softly, as though that would prevent the stairs from collapsing. The walls are a dirty mustard color.

The desk clerk opens the room I've been assigned to, puts my bag on the floor, and leaves without a word. I look around at walls that might have been yellow once upon a time and wonder if things might be crawling in the room that will jump at me. The floral bedcover looks dirty, too.

I hold tight to my handbag, not wanting to throw it on the dirty bed. Next to it are a small table and a small wooden chair. There's dust on the table. Should I just leave? Call a taxi and go to a hotel?

I'm very tired. I mull the options over in my head, and

at the end I'm even more tired. I decide to just steel myself and sleep here. After all, it's just one night. I decide to look at it as adventure.

My body is stiff, and I realize I've been holding my breath. I take a quick inhale. There's a musty, dirty smell in the air. This place is only two or three blocks from the ocean; I wish I could smell the salt air.

The bathroom, unsurprisingly, is not very clean either. I grab some toilet paper and wipe down the table and chair. Then I take wipes out of my handbag—which I still haven't put down—and wipe the table and chair several more times. Finally satisfied, I lay my handbag on the table.

I look at the small brown armchair and decide I'm never going to sit on it. How am I going to sleep? I look under the bedcover. There's one sheet that used to be white. I know I'm not going to get into that bed.

I decide to take a long walk to wear myself out physically—partly so I can collapse and not lie awake worrying all night, but also to see the ocean and the beach. One block away from the hostel, I see a white policeman walking with a foreign white family, clearly tourists. As I slow down and walk behind them, I hear the white policeman saying, "Most of us are leaving. We can't take it anymore." The man of the family asks if he grew up here, and the policeman answers, "I was born elsewhere, but I grew up here, came as a child."

Hearing this makes me stiffen. When I was younger, this was the kind of white person we used to resent and despise, because these are people who came to South Africa during those awful apartheid days when even the most untalented white people could do well in South Africa—at the expense of the black majority. That the apartheid government would subsidize unskilled white people like this policeman's parents, who took jobs that black people could do, was a sore point for us. The apartheid government mounted intensive recruitment campaigns in Europe in an attempt to boost the number of white people in South Africa during those years.

I slow down even more and continue to walk behind them. At the corner, a police car stops and one of the policemen inside leans out and shouts, "Tell them about the couple with the young child."

Another scam, I suspect. Maybe the couple is using the child to beg or something.

At the ocean, I stand alone and breathe in deep to inhale the ocean air. I sit on a bench for a while and watch the setting of the sun. It's a soft orange color. But I have to hurry back to the hostel before it gets dark.

Back at the hostel, I sit on the creaky couch in the lobby, where two young men are watching a movie on the television. It's a Steven Seagal movie. I get my little journal out of my bag and start writing. I don't follow the movie, but occasionally I look up. One of the two young men goes upstairs. I keep my head down, too tired to strike up conversation with the remaining man.

After a while, I look at the time. It's still early, only 11:00 p.m. I begin to think it might be better to just sleep sitting here in the lobby, but after midnight I drag myself to my room. I think about taking out my yoga mat, laying it on the floor, and sleeping on it. But then I see how filthy the floor is. I couldn't stand sleeping on it. So I sit on the chair—bad as it is, it's better than the bed—lay my head on the table, and attempt to sleep in that position. But I don't really fall asleep. I drift in and out of different states of wakefulness. This night is one of the longest I've had in a long time.

MONDAY, FEBRUARY 23, 2004.
Durban to Port Elizabeth.

Morning finally arrives, and I wash my face with a lotion. I'll wash with real soap and water when I get to Port Elizabeth. I go out on the balcony that runs the length of the building on my floor and see a young black woman sitting on a chair. She's reading a thick book that looks like a textbook and taking notes. I guess she's a student, so I don't wish to disturb her, but I wish I could offer some words of encouragement.

I look at my watch; it is 6:00 a.m. I go back into the room and examine my bags and body thoroughly, afraid I might have attracted some kind of bug. I console myself by recalling that I did not even sit on the bed. But my body is itchy.

I go downstairs with my bags and wait in the lobby until six forty-five, when the Baz Bus comes. There's only one driver today, a young Coloured man, and he is very friendly. I'm the first person in the minibus, and I tell him about my experience with the youth hostel and suggest that his company take it off its list of recommended places and pickup spots. He says he sympathizes, but they (the drivers) are instructed not to recommend youth hostels so there's no favoritism to upset the owners.

Our first stop is at a lodge in the suburbs, ten minutes away. I can tell from the outside that it is very nice. We stop and pick up several young European backpackers. After we pick up two more people at another hostel, we're on our way.

At a traffic light, we stop behind a van taxi full of either

Indian or Coloured people—I can't tell. There's a sticker on the back of the taxi: "The Bin Laddin." I expect someone to comment, but nobody says anything. The driver and I are probably the only South Africans in the bus. I remember 9/11—it only happened three years ago, after all—but I'm too exhausted to think about anything.

In a short while we are out of the city of Durban and driving along the east coast. The vegetation is lush with many plants, including palm trees.

We stop for lunch at Stan's Café in Port Shepstone. There's a stack of newspapers near the door. The local paper's headline expresses alarm: ANOTHER LAND CLAIM THREATENS 800 ACRES. The land issue is controversial.

From Port Shepstone, the hills rise and fall and the road climbs up and down. The waves of the land seem to echo the waves of the ocean. The driver tells us we are headed toward Kokstad, where we'll take a ten-minute break and then be on our way out of Natal Province. He says it's going to be a rough ride in the Transkei.

We go through the village of Qumbu, and I am reminded of the story of Nongqawuse. In 1856, Nongqawuse, a teenage girl, went to fetch water, and on her return she told the people of her village that the spirits of the ancestors had said they should destroy their cattle and goods; if they did, the spirits would return and drive the British settlers into the ocean. The people listened, and most of them destroyed their cattle and food. Then they waited for the fulfillment of the prophecy. But the sun did not turn red on February 18, 1857, as expected, and the prophecy was not realized. About forty thousand people died from hunger, and many more were displaced as they left in search of food.

Dennis and Christel, two young people from Holland who are traveling together, strike up a conversation with me, and I soften. I tell them my name once and they pronounce it back perfectly. When they pronounce the g sound perfectly, I ask them if they speak a language that has the same sound. I add that Hebrew has the sound, and people who speak Hebrew pronounce my name perfectly. Dennis smiles and says no, he does not speak Hebrew, but his father is Jewish and his mother Dutch.

We talk about Jewish culture, and they are surprised I know as much as I do. I don't tell them why because I'm more interested in hearing about them. They say they had their first Shabbat in Australia. Then we talk about American politics, which they seem to know a lot about. Later, they get off at Coffee Bay and are picked up by the people of Coffee Bay Backpackers.

A few people get off in Umtata and a few get on. A loud young woman in front says, "You'll love Cape Town. It's not like Africa, it's just like LA." I listen carefully as she continues, "The men are gorgeous, but they're all gay." I do not ask her why she'd bother traveling all the way from the United States to South Africa if all she wants is to be in an American city.

As I smile inwardly, I remember some of the conversations I've had with my students about travel abroad and differences between young American and European tourists. I remember that a South African university official whose office deals with foreign students once told me Americans were the most difficult foreigners to deal with. "They want to come to South Africa," he said, "but they also want everything to be exactly like in America." He said European students adjust and expect things to be different in different places. When I told one of my students in the United States this, she said she hung out with European students overseas because they complained less.

I also remember how once, at another South African university, I defended American students and explained that they are used to universities in their own country, which offer what in other countries would be considered luxury student amenities.

I am often willing to criticize America's shortcomings when I am in the United States but tend to emphasize the good about America when I am out of America. And when I'm in South Africa, I am willing to be critical of South Africa, especially when talking to other South Africans because they have a fuller understanding and know the good parts, but when I'm elsewhere (or talking to non-South Africans), I emphasize the good. Nonresidents tend to exaggerate the criticism and end up with a one-sided view of things.

We are caught in traffic in Umtata. There are mini markets on both sides of the road where people are selling all sorts of things, including vegetables, fruit, and old clothes. People inside our Baz Bus (all tourists and, except me, all white) scramble to take pictures. A young woman asks me, "How do you feel when we do this?"

I shrug. "It's none of my business, and the sellers probably don't care."

One of the young men outside poses with raised arms and a big smile.

Ordinarily, I would love to talk with everybody and find out what they think about South Africa, but I haven't slept, so I'm not in the best mood. I decide to avoid further conversation and questions.

The vegetation in the Transkei is not as lush as that in Natal. We go through the small village of Qunu, and the driver stops on the road a short distance from Mandela's house. He explains that we can't stop right across from the house because that would be disrespectful. People get out and take pictures. Mandela's garden is beautiful. The driver says it was designed by the staff of a popular TV show.

Back on the road, the loud young woman says she'd like to live in Cape Town. I feel sorry for my country.

As we go through Butterworth, it is slow going because of long stretches of road construction. The driver jokes that there's road construction all over as the elections approach. Nothing goes on for four years, and then there's a flurry of activity.

We cross the Kei River, leaving the Transkei behind. On the right are old buildings that used to be for border control between the sham state of Transkei and South Africa. The road climbs a mountain, and as we look down at the valley beyond, I'm glad our driver is skillful. We enter Cintsa Bay on the coast and pass some of the holiday chalets before we stop at Buccaneers Backpackers hostel. We all get out and stretch and I look around the hostel. The view of the water is beautiful and the area is unspoiled. I make a mental note to come here one day and have a month-long writing retreat. I wish I could stay here for a few days now. We change drivers, and our new driver is also very friendly.

Around six thirty that evening, we stop in East London and drop off two people at a hostel overlooking the ocean. The waves are high and the water swirls vigorously. We then stop for dinner at a restaurant nearby. On the wall are posters of Marilyn Monroe and old Coca-Cola. I ask one of the young black women who work there what she thinks about the coming elections. She says she's excited and will be voting ANC (African National Congress), of course.

When we enter Port Elizabeth, the harbor lights are gleaming. We drop off a few people at a guesthouse, and then stop at the Holiday Inn. I get out and see that the driver is also out. Earlier, he promised me he would call my friend Irene to tell her where to pick me up. Now I hear him say into his phone, "Irene, is that your car behind us?"

I'm touched. He's been so helpful.

We walk together to Irene's car and I introduce them, then I thank the driver, shake hands with him, and tell him

I hope to see him as I continue my journey in a few weeks. He writes his full name and telephone number on a piece of paper and says to call him with any questions, and if I need help or wish to know his schedule on this route.

I'm glad to see Irene, an old friend. We met when we were both nineteen. Her former husband, Zondi, grew up in my Mamelodi and was a year ahead of me in Mamelodi High School. Irene, who is from Kimberley, was a nursing student at a hospital nearby. When Irene and Zondi got married in a church, I stood as witness for her and another friend stood as witness for Zondi. We've been close friends ever since, and have remained friends though she and Zondi divorced some time ago.

She takes me to her home, where we sit on her bed and talk for an hour and a half. Now I'm wide-awake and energized. Irene is the chief academic officer of a university and has a meeting tomorrow morning. Feeling guilty, I tell her we have to go to bed.

"You have to get up early, but I can sleep until late," I say. "It's not fair to you."

"It's fine," she says. "Eight thirty is not so bad."

"Really, it's not fair," I insist. "I'll sleep until noon tomorrow."

She just laughs. "I know you, you'll be up at five thirty like you're a farmer."

It's 1:00 a.m. by the time we go to bed.

TUESDAY, FEBRUARY 24, 2004.
Port Elizabeth.

In the morning, I walk the one and a half miles along the road that runs by the ocean to the shopping center and go into Spar supermarket. I see a notice for yoga classes on the notice board in the store. Just what I need. I take down the information. Then I take the long way back to Irene's house. I'm surprised to see all the houses being built in a new development, a gated community. The last time I was here, three years ago, this was all barren land. Now there's no open land between Irene's house and the university. A big board says prices start at R850,000. Luxury housing is booming in this area, which is one of the two poorest provinces in South Africa. I'm reminded of the widening gap between rich and poor in South Africa.

WEDNESDAY, FEBRUARY 25, 2004.
Port Elizabeth.

This morning Irene is getting ready to travel to Johannesburg and, later tomorrow, to Durban for work-related meetings. I will stay in her house while she's gone.

A college car comes to pick her up and take her to the airport. I retire to the study to read and reply to email messages. There's a lot in my in-box, so it takes me two hours. I spend the rest of the day reading.

FRIDAY, FEBRUARY 27, 2004.
Port Elizabeth.

This afternoon I take the bus to the main Port Elizabeth library and am disappointed to find it closed. The notice on the door says it closes at 1:00 p.m. on Fridays. There's also a notice warning people to be careful with their valuables, especially cell phones, as there's been a thief working the library.

I take the bus back to Irene's house and get off at the small mall at Summerstrand. I go to the store and buy the *Mail & Guardian* and the *Sowetan*, another important South African newspaper. I look at the *Sowetan* to make sure it's today's paper, then ask the young assistant if today is Friday. She confirms it. I look at the date on the paper and it says "Friday 27 February." Only now do I remember it is my birthday. I think of my parents and how lucky I was to have had them.

The *Sowetan* newspaper reminds me that today is also the anniversary of the death (in 1978) of Professor Mangaliso Robert Sobukwe. There is a long obituary about his life and his role as the president of the Pan Africanist Congress, the anti-apartheid organization that broke off from the ANC. It was the organization that organized and led the Sharpeville protests in March 1960 against the pass laws. The police shot sixty-nine unarmed protesters, most of them in the back. Sobukwe was known as a man of principle and absolute dedication to the struggle for freedom. He was Dimake's leader and hero. The obituary states, "Sobukwe never compromised the true liberation of his people. He was not a leader to be bought to betray his people for any price."

In May 1960, Sobukwe was sentenced to three years in prison. At the end of his sentence, the South African parliament passed a special law called the "Sobukwe Clause," which gave the minister of justice the power to extend Sobukwe's sentence without charge or trial. Sobukwe was sent to Robben Island, where he spent an additional six years without being charged with any crime. On his release from prison in 1969, he was banished to Kimberley, where he lived under house arrest.

Last week, Khotso Seatlholo, one of the leaders of the 1976 Soweto Uprising, died poor and jobless. So many of the people who played important roles in the struggle against apartheid are now forgotten. And the spoils of freedom bypass many who sacrificed their lives in the struggle against apartheid.

In the same issue of the *Sowetan* there is an obituary for Archbishop Denis Hurley, who in 1957 denounced apartheid as "intrinsically evil." As stated in the obituary, "Indeed, on many occasions he joined protests against unjust laws. In the 1960s he drove 400km from Durban to join a small group of priests who had gathered at a rural settlement in northern Natal to express sympathy and support for a community that was being forcibly removed."

SUNDAY, FEBRUARY 29, 2004.
Port Elizabeth.

As I did yesterday, I spend the morning reading and the afternoon knitting. I'm glad when Irene arrives home after seven this evening. Her trip went well. When I ask her about her housekeeper's persistent cough, Irene says she originally suspected TB and took her to see a doctor. Fortunately the woman does not have TB. It's just smoker's cough and chronic bronchitis. I'm surprised to hear that she smokes and tell Irene that I never saw her smoking. She says she hides it because she knows we disapprove. I feel sorry for her.

TUESDAY, MARCH 2, 2004.
Port Elizabeth.

Today I address envelopes for the letters to friends in the United States I wrote yesterday, then take a long walk to Friends Café for breakfast. I find a seat outside overlooking the ocean. Three young women are seated across from me, and one of them takes out a pack of cigarettes and stylishly pulls a slender white stick from the box. One of the others imitates her, then they both caress their cigarettes with their well-manicured nails. Fortunately, we are outside, so I'm not irritated.

After breakfast I go to the computer center at the university, where a technician has converted my Mac files into PC files. From there I go to the Political Science Department to look for one of the lecturers I met when I was last here in 2001. I learn that he's gone and now works for the government. In the Sociology Department, I seek out an acquaintance who was head of the department in 2001. I'm told she no longer works here; she works for the government now, and is based in Cape Town.

Outside, I run into a Botswana student I first met in 2001. She's excited to see me.

"Is this your last year?" I ask.

"Next year will be my last," she says, then excitedly tells me she visited Michigan during the December-January break at the invitation of a friend who spent a semester here the previous year. "I was so excited when it snowed at Christmas, but when it continued to snow, I got tired of it," she admits with a laugh.

"What did it feel like going from a place where it's summer in December to a place where it's winter—especially a winter that is more brutal than any you've ever experienced in South Africa or your own country?" I ask.

She laughs. "I was so excited at the prospect of visiting the United States I didn't care about the weather."

After our conversation, I take a leisurely walk around campus and recall the good time I had here when I led a group of students who were spending the summer at the university. I had an office overlooking the woods, and looking out my window, I often saw springboks. The university frequently boasts that it is the only university in the world located on a game reserve.

SATURDAY, MARCH 6, 2004.
Port Elizabeth.

I'm the only one at home, and when the remote that opens the gate breaks, I can't get out. The gate is too high to climb over. This living behind high walls and security gates is common in middle-class South Africa, where many worry about break-ins. After Irene comes home, we listen to Miles Davis's love album and read the newspapers, she upstairs and I downstairs.

SUNDAY, MARCH 7, 2004.
Port Elizabeth.

In church today, we chuckle when the minister says, "As long as God gives you, I'll ask." This comes after he reminds the congregation that they are the church and they should support the flower, tea and coffee, and other funds. At home after church, Irene and I relax with a pile of newspapers. We also talk about our families, and Irene says it's a pity her mother died a few years ago.

"I wish she was still around to see the results of her children's hard work," she says, looking downcast.

I try to comfort her. "You were already accomplished by the time your mother died. She got to see you succeed."

"Yes, but it would have been fun to bring her to this seaside city so she could rest and be pampered in her daughter's house," Irene says.

We are quiet for a while, and I remember that this beautiful city is the place where, in 1977, Steven Biko was pummeled by security police and driven unconscious and naked all the way to a notorious Pretoria prison, where he died. The Eastern Cape Province was notorious for having the most brutal security police. It was said that rogue security police were sent to this province.

MONDAY, MARCH 8, 2004.
Port Elizabeth.

I take the bus to a yoga class. After the forty-five-minute session, I take another bus to the university—only to realize I've left my yoga mat in the bus. I take yet another bus, this one to the central bus stop in town, go into the office, and tell a supervisor about my mat. I tell him what bus I was riding, and he checks his schedule and asks me to wait while he calls the driver and asks him if there was a yoga mat left in the bus at the end of that run. After he hangs up, he tells me the mat's not there.

"It's a pity," the other supervisor, who's standing nearby, says.

I smile. "Don't worry. It is a very old yoga mat, that's why I didn't think anybody had taken it."

He chuckles. "You'd be surprised."

We all laugh.

"Well," I say with a shrug, "I hope whoever took my mat gets good use out of it."

They both smile; I thank them and leave. I'm surprised at how little I'm bothered by the fact that I lost my mat.

Next I take a bus to the university. It's a beautiful day, so I decide to go to the library building, where I sit at one of the picnic tables under the trees in front. When I hear a rustling sound behind me, I look and see three monkeys eating scraps of food near some bright orange crane bird flowers. The students sitting at the other tables just go about their business. Most of them are eating. Soon I hear a beautiful whistling sound, and when I look, there's a black bird with a long tail sitting on the cement border across from where I'm sitting. I make a mental note to ask someone the name of this bird.

This is definitely the most beautiful campus in the world, situated in a nature reserve. Around me are students from different backgrounds. At the table next to me sits an Asian student, and at the table next to his are three students speaking Setswana, my language. I can tell they are from Botswana. Near them there's a group of white students speaking English. On a bench nearby sit African students speaking Xhosa. One of them is smoking. I remember how in the not-so-long-distant past a young African woman like her would never have smoked, especially in public. White women could smoke and look cool, but black women smoking were suspected of being immoral in many ways. But I guess we are free now . . . free like whites to adopt self-killing practices like smoking.

At another table is a group of Indian students. I appreciate this scene at a university that used to be whites-only.

A white male student sits down at the now-empty table next to me and opens a plastic container filled with rice and vegetables. He looks at me and smiles, and before he can avert his friendly gaze, I ask him if he knows the name of the black bird with the long tail that was sitting on a tree limb a little while ago. I add that it had a sweet song.

He smiles. "Yes, I know it, it's got a long tail." He thinks. "I see it all the time," he says, "but don't know its name."

"Thank you anyway," I say. "Maybe I'll go to the Zoology Department to ask."

He laughs. "They'd like to help, I'm sure."

When he is joined by another student, Indian, I cock my ear in their direction. They talk about one of their courses. The Indian student says he worked on the reading for the logic course for quite a while. The white student says he also worked hard on it over the weekend. The teacher in me loves this conversation and I'm tempted to tell them I took two logic courses as an undergraduate, but I restrain myself.

TUESDAY, MARCH 9, 2004.
Port Elizabeth.

I get up early and open the window. When the alarm shrieks, it takes me a moment to realize it is triggered by the window. I open the bedroom door and go out and find Irene already standing at the alarm keypad disarming it. The phone rings, and she answers and explains that her guest forgot and opened a window before disarming the alarm. When I apologize, she says it's nothing.

"I sometimes forget and open a door or a window without first disarming the alarm," she reassures me. "But you know, if I'd sounded the least bit nervous on the phone, the security people would have been here in minutes."

Given the level of crime here, this is a comforting thought. Sure enough, a few moments later an ADT car goes by slowly.

Irene's housekeeper, Sisi, joins us and tells me that once when she first came to live with Irene, she was alone in the house and the alarm went off. She didn't answer the phone, and in three or four minutes, the security people arrived. They leapt over the high gate and knocked hard on the door. When she opened the door, they had their guns drawn. She said the incident made her feel safe because she realized just how speedily they respond, faster than the police.

The security business is one of the fastest-growing businesses in South Africa; everyone who can afford it registers with a security company. Gated communities have their own extensive security operations, and a lot of people trust them more than they trust the police. It is almost as if there are two parallel security forces.

I take a black taxi to a yoga class a few miles away. The driver races with another driver on the busy road in their struggle to be ahead so as to pick up more customers. The driver's helper, who is sitting in front next to the driver, sticks half his body out the window and shouts, "Town, town!" calling out for potential customers. I am afraid he might fall out, as he's holding on with one arm while pointing toward town with the other. Meanwhile, the driver is recklessly weaving in and out between cars. I'm terrified! I look around to see if other people are also scared. I regret not having waited for the bus. *Better late than never*, I think, and wonder if I should get out of the taxi; I'm only about a mile from the yoga studio.

The taxi suddenly starts rattling. The driver pulls off the road and stops. I take a deep breath. The driver says it's a breakdown, and we should get out and take another taxi. He also refunds our fares.

Since I'm near where I'm going, I consider not taking back my money, but then I remember how terrifying this short trip has been and decide the driver deserves neither such consideration nor my kindness. I make a mental note to give the fare amount to someone who deserves it.

I walk the short distance to my yoga class. Still shaken by my taxi ride, I really need and deserve yoga today. I wish there was a black person in the class with whom I could share my latest taxi story, someone who has taken a black taxi and understands from personal experience and not just hearing about it or seeing the rough driving on the road.

Still, the short opening meditation calms me.

In the staff lunchroom at the University of Port Elizabeth, I meet a young woman named Thoko. On finding out I'm a political scientist, she becomes excited and tells me she wants to study international relations. She has a graduate degree in linguistics and she is interested in international relations. She says she's glad to meet me because I know about what she's interested in.

After lunch, I decide to walk back to Irene's house, a two- or three-mile distance. Along the way, I meet a young woman carrying two book bags, one in each hand. We exchange greetings and pleasantries, and I ask how far she's going. It turns out she's going only a few houses from Irene's house, so we walk slowly together.

"This is a long walk for someone carrying so many books," I say.

"We are used to it," she says. "I could not find accommodation on or near campus."

"It must be hard," I say.

"It is," she says. "Accommodation in this area is very expensive. Some of these houses in this expensive area are rented by students."

"It is a very expensive area," I say. "It has to be more convenient to live on campus."

"Eleven students rent the house where I live, and we share bedrooms," she explains.

"Don't worry," I say, "you will finish and all this will be behind you. And the distance is not bad. I hear many students live in the townships because it is cheaper, but the commute must be a killer."

A white male student on a bike goes by.

"Look," the girl says. "Have you noticed white students and foreign students ride bikes?"

"Yes," I say.

"Black students, even the ones from middle-class families, do not ride bikes," she says.

I smile. "Do you know how to ride a bike?"

"No," she says. "My brothers rode bikes though."

"You can still learn, you know."

She stops for a moment, smiles, and faces me. "Mm. It would be nice to ride a bike here."

"It is fun," I say. "My younger brother, Kabelo, and I shared a bicycle when we were kids, and we often broke the rules and rode on the township's main street with all the buses and taxis. Our mother threatened, many times, to take away our bike if we broke the rules again. One day I had a near miss—I was nearly hit by a taxi—and someone who saw me told my mother. Not too long after that, I hit a fence and fell off and the bicycle was seriously damaged. It was trashed, and my brother and I never got another bicycle."

The girl laughs. "I don't blame her, she was worried about your safety."

"You are so right," I say. "But in fairness to my mother, if we'd asked for bicycles when we were a bit older, she would have bought some for us."

When we reached Irene's house, I bid the girl good-bye. "I hope you are not going too much farther."

"Thank you," she says. "Just around the corner. Not far when I'm not carrying books."

"Thank you for walking with me," I say. "I enjoyed your company and hope to see you again soon. I'd like to hear more about your program."

"Thank you so much," she says. "I did not even feel the weight of the books."

WEDNESDAY, MARCH 17, 2004.
Port Elizabeth.

I take a bus to the Internet café. On the way back, I wait for a bus, but when it doesn't come, I eventually give up waiting and hop in a taxi to the university. The taxi driver is speaking on his cell phone, but at least he's driving within the speed limit. I spend the rest of the day at the university's library looking up some statistics.

FRIDAY, MARCH 19, 2004.
Port Elizabeth.

At 7:00 a.m., my friend Paul, who is an Afrikaner and teaches part-time at the University of Port Elizabeth, picks me up for a trip to Grahamstown, a city that was established in 1820 by English settlers. He'll be interviewing for a job at Rhodes University. Rhodes University is named after Cecil Rhodes, the same Rhodes of the Rhodes scholarship.

Within twenty minutes we are out of the city and on a road that goes through farms. There isn't much traffic.

At Rhodes University, we park and agree to meet back at the car at 1:00 p.m. I enter Rhodes through the arch and ask a young black woman where the library is. She says, "Wait," and runs to a man riding a lawn mower to ask him. I then ask a passing white woman, who answers that she's going that way.

"Thank you," I call to the black woman as she walks back over to me. "This woman says she'll show me the way."

"I'm glad," she says. "The man's directions were not good! I was going to offer to walk with you to help you find it."

I thank her again and tell her I appreciate her special efforts to help me. Then I go with the white woman who's going that way, and as we walk, I tell her how I marvel at the helpfulness and kindness of people and explain how the other woman had run to ask the man mowing the lawn.

"The world is full of wonderful people," she replies, and then she asks if I'm visiting the university. When I explain the purpose of my visit, she suggests that I visit the science exhibition at a building nearby. We part at the entrance to the library. I browse around the library for a while and then stroll around town.

When we meet back at the car at one, Paul tells me he's been offered the job. I congratulate him and tell him I somehow knew he was going to get it. I could not imagine anybody more qualified. He relates how he left the interview room, and ten minutes later his cell phone rang and they called him back to offer him the job and invite him to lunch. He adds that he came to meet me at the car to tell me the good news in person and to tell me to go ahead and enjoy the city for another two hours since he has to go back and meet with the interview committee again and work out some details.

Paul goes back to the committee and I walk along High Street, where I meet Frank, a friend who used to teach at the University of Port Elizabeth and now teaches here at Rhodes. I tell him I went to look for him at his old department, and the person I spoke with there was very rude and unhelpful. Frank says Rhodes is the right place for him, given his academic interests. I tell him that everybody I talked to at the University of Port Elizabeth said the merger with Port Elizabeth Technikon coming next year has demoralized a lot of people, and the place is barely functioning; everybody is just waiting to see what happens next year when the merger takes effect. Many people are nervous. (They are now all part of the Nelson Mandela Metropolitan University.)

Frank laughs and talks about how well-mannered the Technikon is and how maybe they should have the Technikon take over Port Elizabeth University rather than merge with it.

Paul is back at the car at the agreed-upon time, but says he'll be gone another forty-five minutes because they are going to show him his office and introduce him to his staff. I sit on a bench and read the local newspaper.

We leave as soon as Paul returns from his tour and introductions, and it's a breezy, easy drive as we talk about his new job. We stop at a well-known road café and buy their famous *rooster koekies*, an Afrikaner specialty: biscuits cooked on the grill rather than in the oven. We detour to a suburb near Port Elizabeth and stop at Paul's sister's house to tell her the good news about his new job and give them some *rooster koekies*.

Before we get to his sister's house, Paul warns me that his niece may not be able to converse in English. I say English is not our true language and assure him that I love talking to kids and understand enough Afrikaans to have a meaningful conversation with his niece. He does not know that my Afrikaans used to be very good, but I don't say anything about that, nor about how I've not completely overcome my dislike of it as a language of oppression. I can read it so well, however, that I was able to read texts by Afrikaner intellectuals while doing research in graduate school in the early eighties.

I find it difficult to speak Afrikaans with Afrikaner adults, but with a child it is easy. I've come a long way now. I can hear it spoken and not feel any anger or negativity. The curious thing is that even in the old days, when I hated it, I could easily make exceptions when I knew for sure that the speaker or writer was a decent human being and anti-apartheid. I could read the poetry of someone like Breyten Breytenbach and be touched as one human being to another.

I also surprised myself once in the first year of independence when I found myself voluntarily switching from English to Afrikaans when I was visiting my nephew, who worked in the mining town of Thabazimbi.

I had taken a walk in the small town, and as I stood admiring something in a store window, a white woman greeted me and said she liked my striped black-and-white blouse. It was beautiful and unlike anything she'd seen before. She said it was casual but elegant and it suited my warm character. I laughed and said, "Or no, I'm not as nice as you think." She laughed and said, "I can't be fooled. I can sense a warm soul." As she struggled to find a particular word, I almost automatically switched to Afrikaans and joked that my head might swell up if she went on about me. When she laughed harder and louder, I caught a few white people around looking at us strangely. The woman and I continued to make small talk, and she asked where I came from. I told her Pretoria, then expressed my regret that I had to run; it was time to meet my nephew, my reason for being in Thabazimbi, for lunch. She and I shook hands, and as I ran off, she said she hoped to see me around.

It was a very small town, and I was going to be there for two weeks, so I expected to run into the woman sometime, but that did not happen. Still, meeting her enriched my memories of my visit to Thabazimbi, which is one of the small South Afrikaner towns that were generally known as bastions of hard, cruel Afrikaners in the past.

As I bask in my memories, Paul calls his sister on his cell phone to say we are approaching the gate. It opens electronically, and his niece runs over to greet him. When Paul introduces me to her in English, I greet the child in Afrikaans and say how happy I am to meet her and that her uncle told me she was a great kid. I'm proud and pleasantly surprised that I can still speak Afrikaans reasonably well.

When we get into the house, Paul's sister greets me warmly in English and I reply in English. For the rest of our visit, I continue to speak to the sister in English and the child in Afrikaans. The sister is warm. I congratulate her on her fine wooden floors, and she tells me the house is new. They've only been in it for six weeks. I also learn that she's just had a biopsy and the results are not back. I wish her well, and then we talk about our families. Paul explains that her daughter is named after his mother.

After tea we say our good-byes, and when we arrive back in Port Elizabeth, Paul drops me off at Irene's gate. I thank him for a perfect, relaxing, and happy day. I'm glad he got the job.

SATURDAY, MARCH 20, 2004.
Port Elizabeth.

I'm standing at the bus stop when a young man joins me and asks if I'm waiting for a taxi. I'm waiting for a bus, I tell him. Taxis have been scarce.

"Where are you from?" he asks.

"Pretoria." I smile. "Is my accent when I'm speaking Xhosa that bad?"

He laughs. "No, it's not too bad. I could just detect a little something in your voice."

I thank him for being kind.

"You're Sotho," he says.

"Motswana," I reply.

When I ask him about the upcoming elections, he says he'll vote ANC because there's no choice. When I ask if there's a chance he might consider one of the smaller parties, he says it would be a wasted vote because the many smaller parties don't stand a chance. I ask him about the government's delivery of services, and he says it's very bad. It's not the central government, he argues, but the provincial government that's the problem. I say it's a pity that so many people consider the Eastern Cape Province to be the most incompetent and corrupt, given that it is Mandela's home and the second president, Mbeki, also comes from this province. I'm enjoying our political conversation and am disappointed when a taxi approaches and he flags it down and gets in.

TUESDAY, MARCH 23, 2004.
Port Elizabeth.

I'm going to court today, but not for a regular court case.

In 1989, during the apartheid era, three policemen—Constable Mgoduka, Constable Mapipa, and Sergeant Amos Faku—and an *askari* (a turned former freedom fighter) named Mr. Jack were killed by a car bomb in Motherwell, a Port Elizabeth township.

The unmarked car they were in had been given to them by former security policeman Gideon Niewoudt, the man who was in the papers when I was staying with Mathabo in Pietermaritzburg. (My favorite uncle's name is Gideon, and I hate it that my kind uncle shares a name with such a monster.)

In this case, another former security policeman, Wahl du Toit, made the explosives, and Niewoudt detonated the car bomb with a remote-control device. Marthinus Ras was also involved. The order to kill the men had come from the notorious Vlakplaas commander, Eugene de Kock, also known as Prime Evil, who is now in a Pretoria prison.

In 1996, although Niewoudt, Ras, and Wahl du Toit pled not guilty in a court, they were convicted of the Motherwell bombings. They later appeared before the Truth and Reconciliation Commission (TRC) to apply for amnesty, which was denied, with the TRC arguing that they had not disclosed the whole truth. Amnesty was to be granted only to perpetrators who were deemed to have revealed the whole truth about their crimes. So the three men applied to the high court to force the TRC to hear their case again, and their appeal was successful.

This morning I get off the bus in front of the library in Port Elizabeth and ask the security man at the library entrance where the Port Elizabeth High Court is located. He advises me to take a taxi and tell the driver I'm going to the New Law Courts. When I explain I want the High Court, he says it's all there in that location.

I squish into a taxi with about eight other people and get to the New Law Courts. But after I tell an official what case I am there for, he tells me I'm in the wrong court. He advises me to go back to the Information Center in town. The court I'm looking for is two blocks from there. He's sympathetic and says I should always go to the Information Center so I get the right information. I thank him and rush to get back to town.

I'm relieved when I get to court and learn they are running late. Knowing that I'm going to see three of the most brutal apartheid security police murderers, I feel a shiver. Could one of them be among the men who tortured my brother Dimake in a Pretoria prison many years ago?

I'm surprised by how few people are present in this small court. I'm joined in the back row by three women and two men. I assume—correctly, it turns out—that they are the families of the murdered people the hearings are about. I also suspect the young man sitting next to me is the son of one of the **murdered men**. One of the women is his mother, a widow to apartheid murder. In the row in front of us sit four black men, one of whom says loudly in Xhosa, "Some things cannot be forgiven." The people in my row speak more softly. A few reporters sit in front of us.

It is noon, and the court has still not convened. Now a court official announces the court will convene at 2:00 p.m.

A few things, he says, have to be worked out. The defense objects to the families of the victims being represented by Advocate Ntsebeza, former investigations chief of the Truth and Reconciliation Commission, who in that capacity had investigated human rights abuses under apartheid. The defense claims this presents a conflict of interest.

With two hours to wait, I go out and grab a quick lunch. I return to the court around one thirty, and I am standing alone when a man approaches and greets me. We shake hands and he asks how I have come to be here. I tell him I am interested in the case, and since I am already in town, I feel it would be good to support the families. I wish there were more of us.

Now I learn this man is the uncle of one of the wives of the murdered men and he is also here to support them. He also confirms that the young man sitting next to me is the son of one of them. He was a baby when his father was killed. His father, the man tells me, was a good man. He also tells me how this young man hit one of the defendants when he came to apologize, a sham apology designed to curry favor with the Truth and Reconciliation Commission so it would grant the murderers amnesty. I've heard about the incident. The man I'm talking with looks in the direction of the accused and jokes, "How come you're not having lunch with Niewoudt?"

I reply, "I don't want to *be* anybody's lunch. He has eaten too many young black people already."

The man laughs.

I've seen Niewoudt's picture on television and I'm surprised to see he looks so gaunt. The man says Niewoudt used to be well built, like a rugby player, but that was during the apartheid years, when Afrikaner security men were powerful and could kill any black person with impunity.

I tell the man that when we were in college, we used to

joke that all these Afrikaner apartheid security men were former rugby players who had failed to make it into the professional leagues and were bitter and took it out on black men. When he laughs, I ask him if he knows about research on white rugby players, and he says no and laughs some more. I assure him that what I am about to tell him is not a joke. Research done by a reputable organization has shown that most rugby players, including high school rugby players, had brain damage, which explains the craziness and absolute ruthlessness and heartlessness of the apartheid security forces.

"It even goes a long way," I add, "toward explaining apartheid itself—a lot of their leaders were brain damaged!"

The man laughs again, his whole body shaking. He extends his hand to shake mine again and says, "My sister, where do you come from? You'll kill me with laughter."

People start going in now, so the man and I go in. We sit in the same places, and I begin a conversation with the young man and ask him how his law studies are going. He and I shake hands, and he says he should finish in a year or so. I wish him luck. I feel sorry for the families of the murdered men. I'm lucky that my brother came out of Robben Island alive.

There are three white lawyers for the three white defendants. Advocate Ntsebeza, who represents the families of the murdered men, says he wants it to be on record that he has had to recuse himself by request of the defense. Although the perpetrators were offered defense by the state, the victims were not. Ntsebeza has agreed to withdraw from the case because, he explains, he does not wish his presence to "taint" the proceedings and lead to the findings being set aside again on appeal by the defendants. If the defendants were granted amnesty, he argues, and the families of the victims were not satisfied that the TRC process was fair, then "there will forever be a perception that does prevail out there that the TRC process was perpetrator-friendly." He concludes by asking for a postponement.

When the TRC chairman-judge asks how Ntsebeza can reconcile state expense and the interests of the families of the victims, Ntsebeza says the issue has serious implications for everyone in South Africa. There's some back and forth between Ntsebeza and the chairman, who says he doesn't think justice would not be served because of who the victims' lawyer is. Ntsebeza still requests a postponement to allow the family time to find another advocate. The defense opposes the application. The chairman calls for a fifteen-minute recess.

During the recess, the defendants stand on one side of the room, conversing jovially with their lawyers. They are all smiles, and I wonder if this is because they don't take seriously the gravity of their actions and these proceedings or whether they are putting up a good front out of pride. I suspect they are confident they will successfully work the system and will not go to jail. The attitude of these white apartheid-era murderers reminds me of a passage in Lynne Duke's book *Mandela, Mobutu, and Me*: "The absence of white humility or contrition never ceased to amaze me. And the prevalence of white arrogance was galling."[1]

The families of their victims are still sitting, composed and somber, in the courtroom. Ntsebeza is standing on one side, talking to the instructing lawyer. Journalists are milling around with notepads and pens.

The chairman comes back and postpones the proceedings until Monday, March 29. I regret that I will have left Port Elizabeth by then.

---

1. Lynne Duke, *Mandela, Mobutu, and Me* (New York: Doubleday, 2003), p. 49.

Outside, I introduce myself to Ntsebeza and tell him I reviewed the book he coauthored, *Unfinished Business*,[2] for an American journal. He's glad to hear this and laments that they seldom see reviews published in the United States. Then he gives me his business card and begs me to please send him a copy of the review. I praise him for all the work he has done with the Truth and Reconciliation Commission.

2. Terry Bell and Dumisa Buhle Ntsebeza, *Unfinished Business: South Africa, Apartheid and Truth* (Observatory, South Africa: Redworks Press, 2001).

WEDNESDAY, MARCH 24, 2004.
Port Elizabeth.

Today I visit the office of the American Study Abroad Program based at the University of Port Elizabeth. The brother of the director is an old friend who went to graduate school in Boston at the same time I did. I find his assistant, a young woman who lives in Brighton, a township in Port Elizabeth, and tell her about one of my former students from the college where I teach near Boston who grew up in Brighton. I visited her family the last time I was here. She says she knows their name. When I tell her about the TRC hearing I attended yesterday, she tells me one of the wives is a relative of hers. I ask about the American Study Abroad Program and how the American students are doing.

"This is a very good group this year," she says. "They all enjoyed their homestays." She laughs. "When I asked one of the American students what's different about South Africa, he said, 'The people are slow here.'"

We both have to laugh at this.

"I hope to visit America one day," she says wistfully.

"It will happen," I say. "We should talk about it some more."

THURSDAY, MARCH 25, 2004.
Port Elizabeth.

After my yoga class I go to the Spar supermarket and read the postings on the big community notice board. I find notice boards interesting. One can learn things about the community from them, or at the very least be entertained by what's posted. I see a handwritten notice in a neat handwriting:

DOMESTIC—TO HIRE—3 TIMES PER WEEK

My very, very reliable domestic, who has never missed work in twelve years, seeks work for three days a week. She is hardworking, trustworthy, and fit, has good values, and does not have any domestic problems at home. She is an absolute lady with a wonderful personality. Only people who will look after her well and treat her well should apply. I pay her R80.00 per day, and she deserves every cent and more!

The notice below hers reads:

5 LITTLE KITTENS NEED GOOD HOME
5 weeks old
They are de-wormed
Mother is black

SUNDAY, MARCH 28, 2004.
Port Elizabeth to Cape Town.

This morning I take the Baz Bus to Cape Town. The garden route between Port Elizabeth and Cape Town is beautiful. I'm the only South African and the only black person on this bus.

Our first stop is Jeffrey's Bay, which is well known for hosting international surfing competitions. We stop at 1:00 p.m. for lunch, and the driver, Brian, a Coloured man, and I eat together. He tells me about his family and two small children and shows me pictures of them. We also talk about how we often don't explore our own country. During apartheid, we know, it was very difficult for black people to travel, but now it's different and I believe we should visit all parts of our country. He says he lives in Cape Town but has never visited Robben Island. When I tell him I have visited Robben Island, he resolves to go there with his family one day.

We arrive in Cape Town in the early evening and settle in at a youth hostel near the harbor.

MONDAY, MARCH 29, 2004.
Cape Town.

I'm glad this youth hostel is just two blocks from the Victoria and Alfred Waterfront and a mile from the center of Cape Town. I'm standing in line at the seafood shop for lunch when I hear the young woman behind me say with an American accent, "Chips is fries, right?"

"You're right," I tell her, and then I add, "I guess in America you'd call them 'freedom fries.'" This name, of course, was made up by an American congressman in 2002 when France refused to join the Iraq War being declared by the Bush-Cheney administration.

The American students laugh and one of them says, "It was so stupid."

"Childish," another says.

"Yes," I reply, "we should just laugh about these things."

They all nod and one of them says, "You're right, otherwise we'll be miserable."

I'm glad they recognized my reference to freedom fries. I also recognize that I'm homesick for America.

Now it is time to catch the boat to Robben Island. The boat, a catamaran, speeds off and the mainland recedes. Table Mountain stands solid and immovable in the distance. I imagine how Dimake must have felt when he was taking this trip to begin his life sentence. This happened a few months before his nineteenth birthday in 1963. How terrified he must have been as they went deeper and deeper into the unknown. I remember it was worse for him because he was in an old boat. I, too, rode in some of those old boats when I came to Robben Island to visit him during his imprisonment.

Dimake and the other prisoners rode in the belly of the boat, shackled, so they did not see the scene I am seeing. I imagine how seasick they must have been. I always feel pain when I visit Robben Island; each time, the harrowing memories of Dimake's years there flood over me and sometimes threaten to drown me.

As the boat sways side to side, I breathe deeply and try to slow my breath. The boat is full of tourists today, and everybody looks happy. I tell myself I should be happy, too. After all, apartheid is defeated, the prison was closed in 1996, and my brother survived . . . though others did not.

In the old days, with the old boats, this used to be a forty-five-minute trip. Now the trip is shorter—only thirty minutes.

The guide who meets the boat on the island introduces himself and says he's a former prisoner.

I ask him to tell us what it was like the day he landed here the first time. What was it like when he got off the boat?

"We were terrified," he says. "We were met by warders with big dogs, and both dogs and warders looked like they were ready to kill us. I didn't think I was going to live. The guards would just beat us up for no reason."

I think of Dimake, and I still feel great anger. I quickly get hold of my emotions, however, and remind myself it's all over.

Next we walk to the cell area, where our first guide introduces another former prisoner, Dan, who will be our guide. Dan tells us how harsh the treatment was, especially in the sixties, and gives us a typical example.

"One day," he says, "a warder was annoyed with John, a political prisoner, so he got some common Coloured prisoners, who lived separate from the political prisoners, to dig a hole and put John in it and cover him with only his head showing. The warder then forced John to open his mouth, and they urinated in it."

He says there were many other, similar incidents of sheer cruelty. He shows us one of the large cells first, and the thin mats that served as mattresses. He says he was cold all the time for many years because they never got enough blankets and the cement floor was freezing, even during summer nights. When he closes the metal door, it makes a jarring noise.

"And I closed it softly," Dan says. "The guards used to bang the doors, especially at night, while we were sleeping. It is still a painful sound."

I feel burning tears inside my eyes, and even though I'm not seeing this for the first time, it hurts afresh.

After Dan leads us to see the single cells where Mandela and his colleagues were kept, we get into the bus to go to another section of the island. On the way, another former prisoner gives us some background about the history of Robben Island. The prison was built on top of a cemetery, he says; about two thousand graves were dug up before construction commenced.

As he's talking, I think of my family's forced removal from Kilnerton when I was a child and how there, too, graves were dug up. One of these was the grave of my maternal grandfather, who died long before I was born. My grandmother talked about how much seeing the dug-up grave hurt. A little electric current seems to go through my heart, and I remind myself again that it's over and I should not hurt.

The guide is now speaking about how before it was an apartheid prison, the island was a leper colony. There was a couple who were separated on the island. They died within one and a half hours of each other.

We stop in front of a tiny house the guide says we will see only from the outside. This is the house where Robert Sobukwe, the man who broke away from the ANC to form and lead the Pan Africanist Congress (PAC), was kept alone for many years after he completed his sentence in the early sixties. Sobukwe had been sentenced after organizing and leading, as president of the PAC, the 1960 Sharpeville protests against the pass laws, which required every black person to carry the hated identity document. Just before his sentence was done, the apartheid parliament passed a special law called the Sobukwe Clause just to keep him on Robben Island legally. His court-imposed sentence had expired, and there was nothing to charge him with under existing law, so they invented something new.

The Sharpeville massacre was reported all over the world, and it galvanized world support against apartheid. Pictures of unarmed protesters shot in the back as they fled from the police were plastered on the front pages of major newspapers all over the world. About 369 people were killed throughout South Africa at that time. Sobukwe was a university lecturer, and it has been said he was the most feared black man in South Africa (by the apartheid government, that is).

The guide tells us Sobukwe was completely isolated and the guards and people who delivered his meals were told never to talk to him or even acknowledge his existence. "You can imagine," he says, "how painful it was knowing that some of your friends were less than a mile away but you could not see them."

I think of Dimake, who was a member of the PAC. Sobukwe was his leader and hero. Once again, I suppress the tears.

The guide also talks about breaking lime at the quarry—how the dust and the glare of the sun reflected on the rock damaged the men's eyes. Yes, I remember how thick my brother's glasses were.

Prisoners made the best of this horrendous situation, and later, when they were allowed to study, most of them pursued education through correspondence courses with a vengeance. They helped each other with their studies. The guide explains that they called the prison The University.

On the way back to the mainland, I sit in the upper deck of the boat, all the way at the back. I'm quiet all the way, my heart heavy with thoughts of my brother's life. I wish he were alive today to take this trip with me. I'm sad and happy at the same time, and my mind swirls like the ocean surrounding me.

Back on the mainland at the waterfront, I walk around and go into the Red Barn, a store that sells household goods. It's not busy, so I have the opportunity to talk with a woman who works there for a few minutes. She says she can't establish her business in the township because there is no business or security there, and she'd be robbed.

I leave her store and walk around a little bit more, then go back to the hostel. I spend the evening in my room, alone with my thoughts. The only company I wish for now is that of one of my surviving brothers.

TUESDAY, MARCH 30, 2004.
Cape Town.

This morning I talk with Jolene, one of the Coloured women who work here in the hostel as a housekeeper. She is as dark as I am but is Coloured in the South African sense, meaning of mixed-race ancestry. Her hair is curly like mine but chemically straightened.

I remember how when I taught South African politics to American students, I took pains to explain the complexity of South African racial classifications. Yes, it was based on color, but it was also complex sometimes. Some black people had lighter skin than many Coloureds, and some Coloureds had darker skins than many black Africans. I tell them about one of the most prominent black political leaders, who had a white father but was not Coloured because he was legally and culturally African. Nobody referred to him as Coloured. I remember how hard it was to make the American students understand that Coloured and African legal identities were completely separate under apartheid. Whatever fluidity between the races had existed in earlier times, it was removed after 1948 by the apartheid government.

Before 1994, one of my African American students, who was lighter than me, followed me out of the room after class and asked me what she would be if she went to South Africa.

"Depending on circumstances," I replied, "you probably would be classified as 'honorary white'—especially if you went as an employee of the American embassy. Or maybe you'd be classified as Coloured."

She got very angry at this. "No," she insisted, "I'd be African."

I later went to lunch with her, and we discussed race in the United States and South Africa. I told her that Africans would accept her fully—that we identified with African Americans and were inspired by their struggles. I also told her how even when they were banned, we managed to find and read writings by people like Malcolm X during apartheid. Like the *samizdat* literature of the Soviet Union, the writings were passed around secretly.

My student laughed. "Now I understand why you go crazy when you think we aren't doing our reading!"

"It's true," I admitted. "I come from a place where too many people could not find the books they needed or wanted to read for too long."

I went on to tell her how I harassed my nieces and nephews, even from across the globe, about reading widely—how I always told them that people in their family had sacrificed a lot for them to have the freedom to read what they liked.

I wish I had more time now with Jolene so I could ask her more questions. I'd ask her if it makes a difference that she is Coloured but dark. I'd ask her about Coloured politics in her area and where she stands on various issues. I also wish I had *The Middle Children*, a book written by a Coloured woman, Rayda Jacobs, who lived overseas. It's about Coloured stories and the issues of identity, and the position occupied by Coloureds in South African society. I make a mental note to mail it to her as a gift later.

While we're talking, Jolene tells me about her two boys, who are teenagers. When I ask her if she's working tomorrow, she says no, that day is her day off from this job—but it's not really a day off, because when she's not working here, she goes to her other job as a char.

"When do you rest?" I ask her.

"I have one weekend off every month when I rest and go to church," she says. "I also get leave for a month once a year." She says she wants to build a two-room extension on her house, and that's part of the reason she works so much.

I apologize for taking her time, thank her, and wish her luck.

I go to browse the craft stores at the waterfront. In one store I see cards embellished with tea bags. They are beautiful and unique. As I stand there examining them, the woman who works there, Zelda, explains how they are made. She comes from Galeshewe, a township in Kimberley, and she tells me that even though she misses Kimberley, she likes it here in Cape Town. She has a younger sister in Kimberley who is in grade eight. She plans to take this sister because her brother is a drug addict and she needs to save the girls. "That is the right thing to do," I assure her, adding I respect her for her decision. A sister is a blessing.

Still in the Victoria and Alfred Waterfront complex, I go into the Kraal Gallery, where I admire the handwoven carpets. When the man who runs it greets me, I tell him that this is a wonderful store and I'll recommend it to my friends when they visit Cape Town.

As we chat, I find out that he went into exile to Tanzania with his parents when he was five years old. The Kraal, he says, is reputed to have done well until the sanctions levied by much of the world against the apartheid government hit. I laugh and tell him that I was one of the people who in the United States campaigned for the sanctions against South Africa. I still remember how happy I was the day the sanctions bill was passed by the US Congress over President Reagan's veto. I'm glad when this store owner says he would have done the same thing. The threat of economic collapse helped convince the apartheid government that change was necessary.

He also tells me about growing up in exile and how he went to the Solomon Mahlangu Freedom College in Tanzania, which was mostly for South African refugees. He's surprised when I tell him I grew up in Mamelodi, where Solomon Mahlangu grew up, and that one of my uncles is a close friend of that family. As a child, Solomon went to the lower primary school where my uncle was principal. There's a beautiful statue to honor Solomon at the entrance to Mamelodi now.

Solomon was a nineteen-year-old student during the 1976 Soweto protests against the forced use of Afrikaans as the language of instruction in schools. Many schoolchildren were shot by the police during the protests, and others were arrested, tortured, and killed in detention. Solomon was one of the thousands of schoolchildren who fled the country and went into exile. In 1977, he and a few friends entered the country clandestinely and were arrested. One of them was killed and another tortured so badly after arrest he was unfit to stand trial. Solomon was arrested and sentenced to death. He was hanged in Pretoria on April 6, 1979. Those were traumatic times.

I tell the gallery owner how one of my brothers spent many years in exile in Tanzania and how he loved that country. I also tell him I plan to help Solomon's mother, a liberation struggle hero in her own right, write her story.

When we part, I thank him, and he invites me to please come again. I tell him I would meet with him for tea after work so we could talk some more, but I will be leaving tomorrow. We exchange contact information, and I promise to stop by next Christmas, when I plan to visit Cape Town again.

WEDNESDAY, MARCH 31, 2004.
Cape Town to Pretoria.

I board the bus to Pretoria in the early afternoon. Once out of the city, I enjoy the open spaces. As we drive farther and farther north and away from Cape Town, we go through sparsely populated areas with very big farms. The hills fold into one another. I'm glad the driver is not going too fast: the mountain roads are narrow and it's a steep decline toward the valley below the road.

I remember seeing a South African commercial in which men prop up the mountain with what looks like cement. In a deep voice, one of them says, "How do you stop a mountain from falling into the ocean?" I imagine if the commercial were set here, it would say, "How do you stop a mountain from falling into the valley?"

After sunset, a brilliant three-quarter moon lights up the sky. The movie *Maid in Manhattan* is playing on the bus, but I would rather look outside most of the time. After a while it looks as though almost everybody else is sleeping. There are few stops along the way, and after midnight we stop in Kimberley, the main diamond area of South Africa. It is here that the first large diamond deposits were discovered.

Kimberley is the home of "the big hole," the diamond mine so called because it is the biggest hole in the world dug by human hands. My paternal grandfather worked there as a young man. He and other young men went to the diamond mines in the early 1900s. As the story goes, when they were asked who their leader was, they said Malepe. Instead of calling himself Marema, my grandfather and his brothers became Malepe, so everybody was called Malepe. When the men got back home, they had official papers referring to them as Malepe, and that is why my grandfather and some of his brothers became Malepe instead of Marema. The story also goes that my grandmother did not mind the new name, as she claimed the Maremas never quite liked or accepted her fully, anyway. (I resolve to visit the big hole one day.)

Kimberley was also home to Sol Plaatje, the first African in South Africa to write an English novel, *Mhudi*. He played an important part in the early years of the ANC. Sobukwe also lived here.

After we leave Kimberley, I drift in and out of sleep. In Johannesburg, we change to a smaller bus, and finally, in the late afternoon, we arrive in Pretoria.

SATURDAY, APRIL 3, 2004.
Mabopane.

Kabelo and I take a township taxi to town, where we are met by Dimake's wife, Ntombi. Together, we continue to Mamelodi to attend the land settlement ceremony. We stop at Uncle Gideon's house, and then we all walk together to the Mamelodi Methodist Church, where I'm happy to see members of the fifty-six Kilnerton families.

The master of ceremonies, a man named Patrick, opens the ceremony and explains the purpose of the gathering, which is to celebrate the settlement of the Kilnerton land claim. He then calls on the Reverend Phaswane to open with prayer and we sing *"Re a go boka Morena"*—"We thank you, Lord."

This church was largely built by people from Kilnerton, including my family. I remember the Reverend Mncube, under whose leadership it was built. He was also a family friend. His son spent five years on Robben Island and died before his parents died. I attend this church when I'm in South Africa because this is my old community. Most of the Kilnerton people settled in Mamelodi after we were forcibly removed from our land.

I feel I'm here today on behalf of both my mother's family and my immediate family. My chest threatens to explode with emotion. Patrick acknowledges some of the guests, including the officials from the Land Commission.

There's a big board in front of the church that says, "Commission on Restitution of Land Rights." As the commissioner gets up and walks toward the lectern, he is welcomed with the hymn "*O re nee go thabela, tse O di ratang ka metlha*," which translates as, "Give us the ability to celebrate the things You like." The commissioner welcomes us in Sesotho and then switches to English. But I'm wondering why he switches to English. All the former Kilnerton people understand Sesotho. Switching to English is something I find irritating. It seems to happen whenever officials or others talk to a gathering of people who speak both their main language and English.

When we came in, I saw a young white woman with a black photographer. I guessed that she must be a reporter from the *Pretoria News*, so maybe that is why they have to speak English.

The issue of language in South Africa is a tricky one. There are always stories doing the rounds. In one of them, a Sesotho-speaking doctor speaks to an educated, Sesotho-speaking woman he knows well about the child she's brought in. The doctor says something funny in Sesotho to the kid to put him at ease, and the mother interjects in Sesotho, "Oh no, Doctor, my son cannot understand or speak Sesotho, he only speaks English."

What is wrong with speaking both languages?

The commissioner talks about how important the issue of land rights is and how emotional it is, too. Land reform, he adds, is important. Canada has been at it for forty years and it's still not done yet. Australia and New Zealand are also grappling with it. He declares we in South Africa are doing fairly well as far as restitution is concerned and "we've done a lot in these ten years." He exhorts us to look at our history of dispossession. We all know the story of our conquest and the loss of our land. He talks about the laws that stripped us of our land, beginning with the 1913 Land Act, when our fertile lands were taken away from us.

It is important for us to know our history, he continues. This lack of knowledge of history is the reason the descendants of the people of Marabastad did not lodge a claim, and it's a shame. He informs us that for Marabastad, only people in Laudium have lodged a claim and adds that if we'd kept our lands, we would now not be paying these exorbitant real estate prices we see today and we'd also have sizable assets.

Next the commissioner recalls how bad the apartheid days were and how even walking on the paved sidewalk in the white areas of cities like Pretoria could be dangerous for African people. He smiles as he says that in the past ten years the government has created enough spaces for us to "walk our country without apology." He pauses here. Then he says this land settlement does not compensate us for what we've lost—not just land, but businesses and other valuable things. If the government were to try to truly compensate us, they would not be able to afford it. He pauses again, then rhetorically asks us what the white role is in this restitution. "It is a matter of justice," he declares.

People like the opposition leader Tony Leon don't talk about reconstruction or restitution, but the story is different for white people, because they benefited from the policies of the previous government. Who should address this? The government alone?

The government of **President Thabo Mbeki** did not cause the problems, he says—it inherited them, and now it is blamed for not solving them. Some people clap at this point, but not as loudly as when he next announces the amount of the settlement: R114,000 per Kilnerton household. Now we jump up and applaud.

The commissioner signs the symbolic check and calls on the representatives of the Kilnerton claimants to come forward. He hands them the check, and we all begin singing

"*Kajeno ke mokete*"—"Today is a celebration." Such vindication, such happiness. I wish my parents were here.

The emcee motions to us to sit down again, but it takes a while.

The local city councilor now stands and speaks in Sesotho. He says the ANC gives title deeds to township residents whose homes were, under the old government, considered to be government property forever. He talks about a ninety-year-old man who just got a title deed and says it is sad that it is just now that he gets his title deed. He repeats that the present government gives title deeds. I know that elections will be held in two weeks, so they are in campaign mode. Not that there's any danger of the ANC not getting a big majority.

The city councilor concludes by saying we should remember those who should have been here and are no longer with us. The minister prays and we sing the Xhosa hymn "*Wa gazulwa nge nxa ya mi*"—"You were persecuted for me." When the minister starts by praying for those who should be here, I think again of my parents. I think of my brother, who spent all those years on Robben Island but did not live to see this day. The forced removal of people from Kilnerton and the closing of Kilnerton High School were among the events that made him go into the struggle against apartheid.

We also sing "*Umhlaba wam wam umhlaba wam, khaulethe umhlaba wam*" ("Give me back my land") as the commissioner and the representatives of the Kilnerton committee gather in front to sign the settlement agreement.

After the signing, the chairman of the Kilnerton committee, Leslie McDooley, rises to speak.

He gives a short history of Kilnerton, which was established in 1883. He talks about the good old days in Kilnerton and the good values that informed the community. People chuckle when he says that when he and his friends were young they were not angels and gives examples of how they were naughty, including how they stole turkey eggs from Smith's farm nearby. I see knowing nods from those who are old enough to have taken part in such thefts as children. He pauses to let what he says sink in . . . and then the smile slowly disappears from his face and he clears his throat.

Now he reminds the audience how the apartheid government took our beloved Kilnerton away from us without consultation or compensation, and how they called us *kaffirs*, a derogatory word for Africans. The room grows quiet. The pain of that theft of our land is still fresh in us, and it will never go away. Leslie says he regrets that our parents are gone—that it is a pity they did not live to see this day, to witness the dawn of a new era of public acknowledgement of this wrong done to us and this attempt at restitution by the government. I feel my own sadness that my parents did not live to see this day. I wish they were here.

Leslie asks us to stand and observe a moment of silence to remember that generation and the people who gave their lives fighting against apartheid. They made this moment possible.

It is not only my parents I am thinking of but also Dimake, who died in 2000. I wish he had lived to see this day. I'm consoled by the fact that at least his children can enjoy the new South Africa.

Leslie is saying we should let this gesture from our new government wipe away our tears of sorrow. Today, he says, is a day of celebration. We can let the tears of joy flow freely down our cheeks.

Now I think of my grandmother, who lost so much. With the destruction of the Kilnerton community, she lost not just her house but also the store she owned in Kilnerton and the farm across the main road where she grew vegetables and fruit. This was a lucrative business that had made it possible for her four children, including my mother, to be educated and become teachers.

Leslie changes gears now and reminds the audience that the election is about two weeks away. He urges everybody to vote for the party that restored our land rights. It is because of them that we now have the constitutional right to own land, he says. He also thanks the people who work for the Land Commission, which processes land claims, and there is loud applause. When he announces that a monument will be built to honor the fifty-six families that were forcibly removed from Kilnerton, the applause is even louder. One thousand rands, he says, will be taken from each family's share of the settlement fund and set aside for the creation of a monument somewhere in the former Kilnerton, which is now called Kiljnerpark. The city, he informs us, has agreed to maintain the monument.

I immediately resolve to come home for the unveiling of the monument.

Leslie concludes his talk by pointing out that it is appropriate that this occasion has taken place in the Methodist Church of Mamelodi, since the people of Kilnerton—our parents and grandparents—built this church, and it helped to keep the community together.

Peter, the emcee, stands and thanks all the officials, leaders, members of the community, and visitors. Then he tells how the committee came together to file a claim. First, they knocked on doors. He was surprised to learn that some descendants of Kilnerton had no faith in the process and thought it was a waste of time and nothing would come of it. But the committee members persevered. The day they filed the claim, it rained very hard. This was inconvenient, but good, too, since rain is a blessing. He looks in the direction of the Land Commission's office for our area and says the commission's office was very helpful and the people of Kilnerton are very grateful. At this, people applaud and some stand.

Speeches ended, we all go downstairs to the church hall

for the reception, and I am glad to see the people I grew up with, including Yola, whose father, Uncle Ginger, was our Sunday school teacher. I remember the songs we sang, especially "Joy, joy, joy, with joy my heart is brimming." I still sing it when I celebrate happy occasions. I also recall "*Wa halalela wa halalela*" ("You are holy, you are holy").

Yola is surprised I still remember these. I tell her I'm grateful to her father for all he did for us when we were little. Hers was the most active family in the church of my childhood. Her uncle Joseph, Ginger's elder brother, was the usher who took care of the children and sat in their section and helped to keep them quiet. Ginger and Joseph's younger brother, Uncle Caleb, was the conductor of the church choir.

I'm also glad to see Sister Khohlisane, whose father was my grandfather's friend. She reminds people around us that I was one of her two flower girls when I was six years old. When she invites me to visit her house before I return to the United States, I assure her that visiting her was my intention all along. I remember how sad it was when I learned her son had committed suicide in her house in Mamelodi and they moved to a new house.

My brother Kabelo, Dimake's wife, Ntombi, and I walk to the main street to catch a taxi to town and then another one to Mabopane.

SUNDAY, APRIL 4, 2004.
Mabopane.

Kabelo tells me that people have been talking about a story they say they saw in last week's paper (but he does not know which paper) about women who rape. He says two women in a car asked a man for directions. When the man started to direct them, one of the women said, "Come with us and show us and then we'll bring you back here." He tried to get in the front of their car, but the door was locked and the woman in the back opened the door and asked him to come and sit with her in the back.

"My husband does not like it when men sit in front with his wife," she said, and they all laughed, the man included.

As soon as the car drove off and turned a corner, the woman in the back pointed a gun at the man and told him to cooperate, otherwise she would shoot him. When they got to the main road, the paper continued, she blindfolded him with a dark scarf and told him to relax—that they would not hurt him if he cooperated. When he asked where they were taking him, she said, "To a fun place."

"Don't kill me, please," the man pleaded.

"Kill such a handsome man?" one of the women said. "We just want to have some fun. Relax."

They drove for a while, and then they stopped and led him into some building. When they removed the blindfold, he was surprised to see they were in a beautiful bedroom with a queen-size bed with white and blue covers and pillows. The drapes on the window were a sharp blue.

"That's a nice hunk!" a voice said.

When he heard this, he turned and saw the two women behind him. They were smiling. "We are going to have fun today . . . mmm," one said as she licked her lips. The other woman told him he was going to "do both of them" and he should take his clothes off. He started to say something, but one of the women covered his mouth.

"Shhh," she said. "Don't pretend you don't like it." She told him to lie down on the bed and relax. Then they made him have sex with both of them the whole night.

In the morning they blindfolded him again, drove for a while, and stopped the car. They let him out and told him to go home. But as the car started to move, they stuck their heads out the windows and shouted, "Welcome to the world of AIDS. We infected you with AIDS."

Then they sped off.

"Is this one of those stories that float around but nobody can point to the authoritative source?" I ask.

"Oh no," Kabelo says. "It is true. You'd be surprised at the strange things going on these days."

"Well, I guess so," I say.

I refrain from being too skeptical, because I do not wish to discourage Kabelo from telling me about the stories doing the rounds in the neighborhood. I have gotten some great ideas for short stories out of them.

MONDAY, APRIL 5, 2004.
Mabopane.

I am pleasantly surprised when Helen comes over. We sit and talk, and thirty minutes later we are joined by her husband, my cousin Solomon. They say a friend of theirs who works at the bank in Johannesburg with their daughter, Mary, urgently needs a live-in maid. They have only one child, a young boy who goes to school, and the maid's quarters are beautiful, not just the more common maid's quarters (one room) but a whole separate cottage, outside, with a bedroom, a living area, a kitchen, and a full bathroom. So Mary went to ask Bessie, who lives with her five children and her mother in a two-room house, if she was interested in the job, and she was surprised by Bessie's negative reaction. Bessie shouted at her that she could not lower her dignity by being a maid.

Solomon says he was surprised that someone who did not finish high school, has no special skills, and struggles to feed her children would react this way in a country with such a high unemployment rate. Helen and Solomon say the prospective employer was offering an above-normal pay. I wonder aloud if maybe in addition to the government child welfare grant, a very small amount, Bessie also receives some support from the fathers of the children.

Helen says, "What fathers?" and I drop the subject, but Solomon says they don't know if there are fathers. They only know that the father of her one-year-old child, her youngest, is a pensioner who depends on government grants for seniors. When I suggest that maybe Bessie does not want to be away from her children, they laugh and Helen says that Bessie's mother is the one raising the children, anyway, and Bessie often goes away for weekends. Then they look at each other and laugh, and Solomon says, "Let's leave things at that. We are not going to tell you things."

"Yes," I say, "I don't want to know." We all laugh.

"Young people don't want to do these kinds of jobs anymore," Solomon says, "jobs that their parents did to support them. And yet they are not serious about school, either."

Later, we drive to the supermarket at a nearby mall. I comment on how expensive food is, and my friends laugh and say that's what everybody says. It is late afternoon when they drop me at home. I thank them for a perfect day.

WEDNESDAY, APRIL 14, 2004.
Mabopane.

Kabelo and I leave to go to the voting station at the school around the corner. We are early and the line is not long, so Kabelo votes quickly. From there we go to the corner store, where I buy three newspapers to see what the commentators are saying about elections. I don't expect anything exciting; it is clear the ruling party, the ANC, is going to win with a big majority.

Later in the evening, we watch television news. We feel excited as we see photos of the voting in various areas.

I tell Kabelo how emotional it was to vote for the first time in 1994, after I'd moved to Boston. A crowd of Americans who had worked in the anti-apartheid struggle were there to cheer us on as we voted.

FRIDAY, APRIL 16, 2004.
Mabopane.

Sinah, who is Kabelo's friend, says she didn't vote for the
ANC, and she's annoyed that her province, Limpopo, did.
She feels this way because the ANC is dominated by Zulus
and Xhosas. "What about us?" she asks. "What about the
Bapedi, Batswana, BaVenda, BaTsonga?"

I am surprised by her sentiment. "It is good to have
many parties," I say. "It keeps the ANC on its toes."

On TV this evening, a reporter interviews a prisoner
who says he voted and adds that he wants the government to
do something about crime. He wants to live in a crime-free
country. Kabelo and I laugh, and he says he loves the irony of
a criminal who is behind bars saying he wants a crime-free
country. I say I wish they'd told us what put him in prison. I
suspect the man being interviewed committed a nonviolent
crime, like stealing—or maybe, given how articulate he is,
he might have committed a white-collar crime, which to him
is not real crime.

Kabelo nods. "Maybe only the violent murderers are
criminals to him."

TUESDAY, APRIL 20, 2004.
Mabopane to Mamelodi to Middelburg Mpumalanga Province.

Auntie Gelane's daughter has passed away. Auntie Gelane was the cousin my mother was closest to, and I remember how as children we enjoyed her visits. Their mothers were sisters. It is under sad circumstances that I look forward to seeing Auntie Gelane, as I plan to attend the funeral in Middelburg.

Not long after I arrive at Uncle Gideon's house in Mamelodi around one o'clock in the afternoon, Rachel, Uncle Israel's daughter, arrives. Eddy, Uncle Gideon's son, then drives us to Middelburg. It is Tuesday and the traffic is not too bad. We talk about that side of the family.

On arriving, about four hours later, we go to the bedroom. Auntie Gelane is sitting near the coffin with six women who have come to sit with her, as is traditional. She starts crying when she sees us. She is especially surprised to see me. "They did not tell me my sister Hilda's daughter was coming," she says. She introduces me to the six women sitting with her and says how she misses my mother.

I sit with them until Rachel comes to get me to join our many cousins at the stoop at the back of the house. I'm glad to meet them. Many of us last saw each other when we were very young and don't remember each other now. When I'm introduced to Zola, one of Auntie Gelane's grandchildren, I tell her I remember her late mother, whom I last saw when I was ten years old. Zola tells me she has heard a lot about me over the years from Auntie Gelane and she's been dying to see me. "Of all the children in your family," she tells me, "you are Auntie's favorite."

We are served dinner. After a while, Zola tells me she'll take Rachel and me to her house, which is a few miles away, to sleep for the night. After helping us, she'll return to Auntie Gelane's house for the night. Then she'll bring us back in the morning.

WEDNESDAY, APRIL 21, 2004.
Middelburg.

When we return to Auntie's home in the morning, the coffin is in the tent and people are singing. They belong to St. John's Apostolic church and their band is performing. The music is moving. I am especially moved when the gathering sings the hymn, "*Ha ba tshela noka ya Jordan ba apolela melato*" ("When they cross the river Jordan their sins are washed away").

The priest gives a brief sermon about crossing to the other side and says the deceased is free now; there's no need to fear because she is with the Lord. A few people chuckle when he says some people are so afraid of death that they are even afraid to touch the coffin.

Next, we drive to the cemetery. As the procession goes by, children along the way sit or kneel.

"I'm surprised to see them do that," I tell Rachel. "In Pretoria, children don't stop or kneel or sit when a funeral procession goes by like we used to do when we were children."

She nods. "In some areas, like here, they still follow the old custom."

Some men stop and take their hats off.

We gather at the gravesite, and during the ceremony, Rachel leans over and whispers, "It's not right to go before your mother. It's too cruel."

I nod in agreement. Children are supposed to bury their parents, not the other way round.

Back at Auntie's house, everybody is fed a full meal of cabbage, potatoes, string beans, carrots, and meat. Later, as we get ready to go back to Mamelodi and then Mabopane, Zola accompanies us to the car.

"Your red apron is beautiful and unique," I tell her.

She smiles. "I make them," she says. "They sell very well. A store in Johannesburg sells a lot of them." Then she takes the apron off and gives it to me.

This was not my intention, but I know better than to refuse the gift. "Thank you," I say. "I'm touched. I'll treasure it."

In the car, as we talk about the relatives we've met, I say I wish it had been a happy occasion like a wedding. When Uncle says weddings are scarce these days, we all laugh. The trip back is smooth, and I'm glad for the time to talk about family with my three relatives.

THURSDAY, APRIL 22, 2004.
Mabopane.

The next morning, as I am on my way to buy newspapers, a woman stops me and asks if I know of anybody who needs help around the house—washing, cleaning, stuff like that.

"I'm sorry," I tell her, "but I don't know anybody who needs help."

She sighs. "I walk from the section behind the mountain to the section across the river, and I'm often tired when I get to work. That is why I asked you if there is something in your section here, which is closer. I cannot afford to take a taxi to where I work."

"Yes, that's a long walk, and the taxis are too expensive," I agree. "Do you work full-time?"

"Yes, I work for this family from Monday to Friday from eight o'clock to five o'clock and make five hundred rands," she says. "I do everything outside and inside, including watching their disabled son, who is twenty-one years old. When I complain about the amount of work and the low pay, they tell me if I don't like it, I can leave and they'll find somebody else."

"I thought eight hundred twenty rands was the legal pay," I say.

She shakes her head and frowns. "They don't care. Besides, they still owe me money for two months' wages, and when I reminded them last week, they said it was too long ago."

All I can do is wish her good luck.

On my way back home, I walk behind two young women who seem to be in their twenties. I hear one saying to the other, "I know you're not going to work today."

"I called in sick," the other says. "I pretended to cough." She demonstrates how she talked on the phone and does the fake cough.

"Why do you do this?" her friend, who is clearly on her way to work, asks.

"I'm just tired," the other one replies.

The first one shakes her head and picks up her pace. Jobs are so hard to find, and here her friend is, playing with her job.

After hearing their exchange, I imagine the second girl must still be living with her parents.

FRIDAY, APRIL 23, 2004.
Mabopane.

When I call South African Airways to change my ticket, I am served by a friendly young man who says his name is Mzwandile Shabangu. I tell him I'm trying to change my return date and I hope the penalty will not be too steep. He chuckles and says, "Let's hope for the best." He asks for my details, and then he says he'll confirm my flight. Later, when they are open in Atlanta, he says, he'll call to see about the cost, "and we'll hope for the best." I thank him for his kind help, and he says he'll see what he can do.

In today's *Business Report*, there is a report that includes letters to the chief executive of South African Airways. Most of them are negative. The writers of these letters must not have been lucky enough to be served by Mzwandile, so I decide to write a letter to the paper about his professionalism, warmth, and politeness.

SATURDAY, APRIL 24, 2004.
Mabopane.

I'm visiting my cousin a few blocks away today. She's not well. She's been suffering from a headache for four months. When I ask her why her doctor has not referred her to a specialist at the hospital, she replies that the doctor said the hospital is very busy and it will take a while for her to be seen. I suggest that she go to the government clinic in the neighborhood, where she may have better luck being referred to the hospital.

A friend of ours who lives in the neighborhood and goes to our church stops by. I ask her how things are going at church, and she says they no longer enjoy going to church because of all the discord and the fighting over all kinds of issues, including money. There is also an intense power struggle going on, she adds, and some people are trying to get rid of the minister. An old friend of mine is one of the people causing problems. I laugh and say I thought he had grown up.

I think the minister is a good one. My parents liked him. He buried both of them, and he was good to us during those difficult two years; he offered us a lot of support. My friend says they are tired of the fighting. They look forward to things in the church returning to a normal and peaceful state. I say the man is a good minister. She and my cousin both agree.

MONDAY, APRIL 26, 2004.
Mabopane.

Dimake's wife, Ntombi, and his son, Lebo, are here visiting. Lebo's close resemblance to his father reminds me of my brother. Since his death in 2000, I've tried to spend as much time as I can with Lebo.

This morning, as we weed around the spinach and beets, Ntombi reminds me how much Dimake loved gardening and how he taught many of their neighbors in Atteridgeville (an hour away) to grow vegetables in their yards. I remind her of my mother's love of gardening and her influence on all of us. I also tell her how in Mamelodi, where we grew up, my mother used to get up early to work in her garden before she went to work. Our house was on a corner, and she planted flowers in front and on the sides of the house, and vegetables, especially spinach and string beans, at the back. We also had two peach trees and a grapevine that produced sweet black grapes and made a shady patch in front of the room attached to the house. The red and yellow roses dominated the front, where my mother also planted carnations and other flowers, depending on the season. Yellow marigolds lined the outside of the fence in front. The path from the gate to the garage was paved, but a narrow strip in the middle was left unpaved. My mother planted small flowers there, ones that did not grow tall.

"Once my father cleared that narrow strip, thinking the flowers were weeds," I tell Ntombi. "He didn't realize that my mother had planted flowers he had not seen before.

When my mother came home that day to find her flowers gone, my father confessed. We laughed when my mother told him they were flowers. He apologized and smiled, and told us to be ashamed of laughing at our father. But when he said good children don't laugh at their fathers, we laughed some more. My mother laughed, too."

My father had broken my mother's rule about not working in the garden without her being present. The only thing she allowed anybody to do in her garden in her absence was to water the plants, and that only in the morning or very late afternoon.

"I remember how beautiful your mother's flowers were," Ntombi says. "I used to love to pick them and make arrangements for the house."

"Oh yes," I recall. "You always arranged them so beautifully."

When my friend Betty, a nurse, comes to visit, Ntombi and I decide we've done enough and it's time to stop. We sit on the back stoop and talk about how things have changed and how they haven't. Betty tells a story about how at the hospital where she works, a predominantly black hospital, a young female colleague told her about her moonlighting experiences. One day this young nurse was called to work at a private, mostly white hospital. They said they were short of one nurse for the night, and she told them she could not take the job because she could not get there at night. They offered to pay for a cab to pick her up in town. The cab ride from town to the hospital was 200 rand.

Betty's colleague had never moonlighted at one of these private white hospitals before, and she was pleased when she got there to find she was assigned only one patient for the night, a middle-aged black man. In that expensive place, she figured, he either had private insurance or was very rich.

A white nurse took her to her patient and left without showing her much. There was a machine that she was not sure how to use. When she asked for help, the white nurse sighed and said she was too busy at the moment. It wasn't hard, she said, and the young nurse would figure it out. She was basically left to her own devices.

Fortunately, the patient was highly educated and understood the machine well, and also knew a lot about his treatment. So they helped each other. The young nurse said that once she figured things out, she was comfortable, and she liked having just one patient. But later, Betty said, when she found the nurses' lounge and made herself some tea, she discovered that she was the only black nurse there, and she felt ignored by the white nurses. When she got back to her regular job the following day and told the other nurses about it, they laughed and said they were neither surprised nor shocked.

"Apartheid is still alive in the hearts of the majority of white people," Betty says.

I feel sad. It must be showing on my face because Betty touches my shoulder and says, "Don't get sad." She smiles. "Let me tell you a funny story."

In this story, which she also heard from a colleague, a white Madam looking at a TV screen is excited. Laughing hard, she calls her maid. "Minah, Minah, come and see this!" She waves the maid in and informs her, "Blacks are killing blacks." Minah comes over to see. She has an awkward smile on her face because she knows from experience this cannot be good; the Madam never calls her to see happy stories of black people on TV or the newspapers. The Madam gleefully says, "We won't have to worry about black people. They are going to kill each other. There'll be only four blacks left in the whole country—maybe one in Limpopo, one in the Cape, and so on. The one in Limpopo will hear that there's three more."

At first I am horrified by this story, but then, as everybody bursts out laughing, I laugh with them. I also shake my head. "It's ridiculous," I say. "Why are we laughing?"

They nod and continue laughing.

"We laugh because we survived," I say.

"It's an old joke," Betty says. "From the eighties."

This makes sense. The eighties were a violent period in our history.

Now I'm reminded of a story I once heard from someone who went to the University of Zululand in the late eighties. This was when Inkatha, the Zulu political party approved by the apartheid government, was active. The University of Zululand was a black government university. Buthelezi, the head of Inkatha and head of the KwaZulu Bantustan, was there to give a speech.

The Bantustan system was established by the apartheid government to force the various black ethnic groups into small, desolate geographic areas where they would supposedly rule themselves and lose all claim to white South Africa, which was more than 80 percent of the country. The majority of the students at the university—like most black people, including the ones who lived in these pseudo-states or future states—were opposed to Buthelezi's organization and his participation in the government's Bantustan system.

While Buthelezi was speaking to a small audience inside, his army of warriors sat outside holding sticks, spears, and cowhide whips. A student overheard a bored Inkatha man ask the one next to him, apparently a supervisor, "*So ze si shaye nini izistudent?*" "When are we going to beat the students?"

Yes, they were impatiently waiting for the order to beat up students, as they often did when students protested at Buthelezi's appearances. They were tired of sitting and waiting.

"Be patient, the students haven't done anything yet," the supervisor said. "Maybe they learned their lesson last time."

After Betty leaves, Ntombi and I join Lebo in the kitchen, where he's squeezing lemons and oranges from the trees at the back of the house. I tell him his father used to love squeezing juice. Later in the afternoon, I walk him and his mother to the main road to catch a taxi back to their home in Atteridgeville. It has been another perfect day.

WEDNESDAY, APRIL 28, 2004.
Mabopane.

The newspapers comment on how Mugabe received warm applause at the Union Building yesterday, despite his having presided over the destruction of the Zimbabwean economy, which then led to many Zimbabweans coming here to South Africa, where they are not welcome in some circles. Most commentators agree that South Africans feel strongly about the land issue and support Mugabe for taking away land from some white farmers.

I listen to the evening news on the radio and find out that the old health minister, my cousin's cousin, has been retained, and the former premier of the Eastern Cape has been brought into the cabinet, even though he presided over a troubled provincial administration before this.

THURSDAY, APRIL 29, 2004.
Mabopane to Midrand.

Kabelo accompanies me to town to meet my friends Mbu and Vin. We stop at an Internet café, where I check my email. I'm glad there are no important messages. I'm excited about meeting my friends and then going with them to the University of Venda, where they work.

Kabelo and I wait at the corner for about two hours. I'm glad when Mbu finally arrives to pick me up. We go to their house in Midrand, twenty-five minutes away, where Vin is waiting. I thank her for inviting me to go to Venda with them.

Vin is special. We've known each other since our first year at Moretele Primary School, when I was four years old. The next year, I transferred to a new primary elementary school, Vulamehlo Lower Primary School, which was a stone's throw from my home. Some years later, our fathers served together on the Mamelodi High School school committee and knew each other well. Vin and I also got Fulbright Scholarships to study in the United States around the same time; though I stayed in the United States at the end of my studies and she went back to apartheid South Africa, we have stayed in touch over the years. Being with her today leads me to reflect on my childhood and early schooling in Mamelodi, where we both grew up.

As in most urban areas of South Africa, the majority of the houses in Vin's neighborhood here in Midrand, between Pretoria and Johannesburg, are surrounded by tall walls that sometimes have barbed wire or an electric fence on top.

"I'm fascinated by houses in the suburbs that don't have the walls or fences," I say. "I noticed that the house just across the street doesn't have any."

"There are a few of those," Mbu says.

"I wish I could talk to those brave souls and ask them why they don't have the high walls," I say. "I wish I could ask the owners how they came to the decision to not surround their house with protective fences. There has to be a story there."

Vin's house is not so unprotected: it is surrounded by a high wall with an electric fence on top. There is also a carport, not a full garage. They say they were robbed last year. The open carport lets burglars see whether the car is there or not. The burglars stole computers, a TV, and other small electronic devices.

Vin tells me she gets along well with her white neighbors across the street and they look out for each other. But she has had problems with the black neighbors next door, who have, among other things, damaged her wall.

FRIDAY, APRIL 30, 2004.
Midrand.

Mbu and I drive to the offices of the National Arts Council near the Market Theatre in Newtown, Johannesburg, where I pick up the forms I need to apply for a research grant. The settlement of our Kilnerton land claim has led me to reflect on life in Kilnerton, and I've decided to write about it, and about the impact the land being taken away had on my family and the Kilnerton community. Mbu, a former literature professor, has offered to write a recommendation for me and feels confident I will get the grant. I knew about him from his brother when I was younger, but I didn't meet him until many years later, when we were both in the United States and were invited to present in a workshop at Boston University. He had gone to school with my cousin in the East Rand, and my aunt and his mother, both nurses, were friends. I feel lucky to have met him and grateful for his support.

Mbu and I talk about the different perspectives of black and white people and about how people are always saying we should forgive—victims are made to bend over backward to do so—while nothing is asked of the perpetrators and beneficiaries of apartheid. There is a story about white mercenaries detained in Zimbabwe, but there isn't much talk about the black community in South Africa. We also talk about how white commentators were happy that Mugabe, the Zimbabwe president, was refused accommodation in some establishments, but when he appeared at the Union Building, black people cheered him loudly, the sound second only to the cheers for Mandela. Mugabe took land from some whites, an action many blacks in South Africa saw as historic justice. That some of his policies led to the decline of the Zimbabwean economy is seen as a separate issue altogether.

In the newspaper, the last president of apartheid South Africa is quoted as lamenting the weakness of the opposition and the dominance of the ANC, "which means no democracy."

"It would have been nice to hear him say while his party dominated South Africa that it was too bad the opposition was weak," I comment.

That president's party, the National Party, was more dominant in his day than the ANC is today. The opposition parties were much weaker back then, and he probably did not mind. Apartheid supporters are still seen as lacking the moral authority to criticize the present government, even when their complaints have merit. Mbu says—tongue in cheek—"Of course now nobody ever supported apartheid."

Our errand completed, we join Vin back at the house and relax for a while. When she goes to get her hair braided, we all go out to a fish restaurant. It's a pleasant place, and because it's midafternoon, it is not crowded. We notice how all the servers seem to be from other African countries and suspect they are underpaid, making it more profitable for the owner.

"It's even better for the employer if his employees are here illegally," I point out, "because then they cannot go to the Labor Department with their complaints. They are afraid of being deported."

SUNDAY, MAY 2, 2004.
Midrand to Thohoyandou.

I am excited today as we get ready to leave for the University of Venda in the Limpopo province in the north. Our drive is uneventful. Traffic on the highway is not heavy, which reminds me of the days when it was a two-lane road.

We pass many small towns. After Pietersburg, the landscape begins to change, becoming more lush, and just as the sun begins to set, we pass the sign for the Tropic of Capricorn. The moon is so bright we can see the hills in the distance. We drive up into the mountains and look down on the distant valley to the left, where Mbu points out the Modjadji area.

I tell Vin and Mbu about the time, a few years after high school, when I drove with a friend named Nobi to take her younger sister to a boarding school in Magoebaskloof, down below in Modjadji. The queen of Modjadji was known to be a rainmaker. I remember how green everything was and how the valley got rain even when the surrounding areas were dry. Nobi and I spent the night there after we dropped off her sister and left the next day. I remember that time fondly.

As we drive past Magoebaskloof, I point to lights in the distance. Vin reminds us how in the past seeing the lights would have meant a white town, but now it could be a small village. The new government has provided a lot of small villages with electricity.

My cell phone rings. It's my brother Kabelo.

"I have bad news, 'Sego," he says when I answer. "Sesi has passed on."

I grew up with Sesi in Mamelodi. Her family lived across the street from us. Her mother stayed home and often sat on the stoop in the late afternoons and watched us play. She was kind, and we children went to her if there was nobody at home.

"I know you're thinking of turning around to come back for her funeral," Kabelo says, "but please don't."

He assures me that he and my other brother will go and help out. He also promises to take me there when I get back and also promises to call me again tomorrow with details.

After hanging up, I tell Vin and Mbu the sad news and how I regret missing the funeral. Vin assures me it is not so bad because other people, like Kabelo, will go.

My eyes feel heavy; tears are suspended in them. I struggle to keep them from falling.

After a while we reach Thohoyandou, where the university is located. I'm looking forward to seeing the area in the daytime.

MONDAY, MAY 3, 2004.
Thohoyandou.

Vin and Mbu go to work at the university. I stay home. I walk around the housing complex and am glad it's warmer here than it is in Pretoria, where winter has already reared its head with chilly air. I'm also glad I'm here at this time of year, when malaria-carrying mosquitoes are not so common.

At the entrance, I greet the security guard. As we chat, he says he knows about me because my hosts have already notified him about my visit.

"The houses in this complex are so spacious and beautiful," I say.

"They were originally built for white academics who worked at the university," he says. "Now it is a university-owned housing complex for faculty and senior staff of all races."

We talk about the weather. I comment that it's pleasant here, much warmer than Johannesburg and Pretoria.

He nods. "Yes, I know. I used to work in Johannesburg. The weather is much better here."

After a bit more small talk, he tells me he hopes I will enjoy my stay, and I go back inside and read the local paper. There's a story about a white man who claims he was fired from his job because he was an ANC member and his employer found ANC recruitment forms in his locker.

TUESDAY, MAY 4, 2004.
Thohoyandou.

I wake up refreshed this morning, greeted by two birds singing outside my window. I look out the window but I don't see them. After Vin and Mbu leave for work, I go outside and greet the man and woman working in the garden. They both understand my language well because they've worked in Johannesburg. I speak Venda a little bit, but have a hard time. I enjoy our conversing in two languages and combining them in interesting ways.

In the newspaper today there is a story about linen being stolen from a hospital. I remember hearing a similar story in Pretoria.

Mbu returns in the afternoon. As we drive around Thohoyandou, we pass many commercial farms with irrigation systems. I ask Mbu if the Land Commission has been active in this area; it seems many people here must have had their land taken away from them without compensation in the past.

"I haven't heard much about the issue here," he says with a shrug. "The white population here is not as big as in our province in the south, and land seems to be abundant, so the issues of land and dispossession are probably not as problematic as in other areas."

We pass many fruit and vegetable stalls, and I notice that the prices are much cheaper than in my home, Pretoria.

"Everything is so inexpensive," I say.

"Yes, there's plenty of food in this area," Mbu says. "In the evenings one can sometimes find vegetables thrown out at the food stalls and outside the farms." He points to the farm we are passing. "This tomato farm, for example, is very productive. Outside the gates, one can often find tomatoes, and people can just take them." He also points to some fruit trees that are growing wild.

We stop at a market and buy mangoes, avocadoes, bananas, pawpaws, and guavas. We also give a ride to a woman with a six-year-old child. When I ask why the child looks sad, she says she's crying for her father, who just left them to go to work. I try to comfort her but she does not respond.

As they're about to get out of our car, the woman extends a R10 note to Mbu.

He refuses it. "Payment is not necessary," he says. "Please, buy something for the child with it."

She thanks us and the little girl smiles and waves good-bye.

Back at the house, I go out for my afternoon walk. When I stop to look at a patch of greens, the guard comes over and greets me.

"Are you admiring the greens?" he asks, smiling. "They are Chinese vegetables."

"Are they really from China?" I ask.

"I think so," he says. "We didn't have them here when I was a child."

"I grew up eating a lot of greens," I tell him.

He laughs. "I would think that living in America, you've forgotten things like traditional greens!"

It's my turn to laugh. "How did you know I live in America?"

"I heard yesterday when I was with the woman who

helps with the gardens," he says. "We are very surprised because you look and act normal, and not like some people who visit America and come back changed. They talk funny and pretend to have forgotten their own languages."

"What do you mean when you say I act 'normal'?" I ask, curious.

"You're friendly," he says. "You stop to greet people."

He adds that he's surprised he never heard an English word from me. Instead I speak my language and make an effort to speak his language too. We go on to talk about vegetables and fruit, and I say I was glad to see big guavas at the market.

"Yes," he says, "I missed the fresh food from here when I went to work in Johannesburg. Here, nobody starves. There's always enough to eat. Even when people don't have material things, they still have good food."

"Food is what's important," I say.

When I comment once again on how mild it is here, unlike in Pretoria, where it is already beginning to get cold, he remembers the brutal Johannesburg winters. When I tell him they are nothing compared to the winters in Boston, where I live, he says he's only heard of snow and freezing weather, never experienced it for himself. Finally, I bid him good-bye and go on with my walk.

In the papers today, there is more about the white mercenaries who were detained in Zimbabwe. A relative of one of them is quoted as asking, "Why can't South Africa fight for these men?"

This is not much of a story in the black community. The few people I've asked about this issue have not shown much interest. Although the government is required to advocate for South Africans in other countries, I imagine there cannot be much enthusiasm for standing up for white mercenaries. Many of them are former soldiers of the former South African army and fought in Angola and Namibia; these are probably the same whites who belonged to the security units that killed so many anti-apartheid activists. And Zimbabwe itself has been terrorized by apartheid government security people. As a young man I talked to in Pretoria said, "I have no sympathy. These are the same people who killed a lot of our people."

WEDNESDAY, MAY 5, 2004.
Thohoyandou.

One of the headlines in *Business Day* reads, LAND ISSUE ILLUSTRATES SOCIAL RIFT. This is just one example of the many issues where European South Africans and Africans see issues differently. In another section there is a story that says, "Just placing women in top posts [is] not empowering."

THURSDAY, MAY 6, 2004.
Thohoyandou.

I hear a knock, and when I open the door, there is the guard I was talking to the other day. He has brought me one large avocado. I understand the gesture; it says, "Welcome to my area."

"It is ripe and ready to eat," he says with a huge smile.

"Thank you," I say, turning it in my hands. "I will definitely eat it today."

I will, in fact, share it with Mbu and Vin, and I appreciate this gesture of generosity from a total stranger. One finds such gestures in areas like these—places that are not completely urbanized.

In the evening, Rose, a neighbor and colleague of Vin and Mbu, joins us for dinner. Rose lived in Baltimore for seventeen years. When I ask her how she came to work here in this area, she says she signed a five-year contract with the university but was not prepared to stay beyond that time. She was at the University of the North in the early seventies. They just had a reunion at the funeral of someone they went to school with. She comments on how family expectations can be a problem.

"Some people try to give me children to look after 'so you have someone to send to the store,'" she says. "To which I reply that I have a car and do not need anybody to go to the store for me."

I've had similar experiences. "Even when you're overseas, they try to get someone to live with you," I say.

"When people say to me, 'God has made a decision, a choice not to give you children,' my response is swift: 'No, no, no—I made a choice, I don't want children.' Which shocks them."

We laugh when she says her favorite is when someone has passed matriculation and wants to go to the university and needs accommodations. "'Let her or him live with you,' they say, 'and they can clean and help you.'" We all laugh. All four of us have spent years living in the United States at one time or another.

Mbu says how he was surprised when not too long after he arrived here in Venda, someone called him aside and said non-Venda people who work here should watch their backs because there is a lot of resentment. Many locals feel that outsiders are taking their jobs. We all laugh and agree the sentiment is universal.

FRIDAY, MAY 7, 2004.
University of Venda, Thohoyandou, Limpopo Province.

I'm glad to be here during graduation weekend. Vin, Mbu, and I go to campus and start our visit at the vice-chancellor's office. Professor Nkondo is happy to see me and says we should get together after graduation and catch up. Next we are led to the graduation hall, where we are seated in the second row, behind the traditional royal family of the area.

"That's Chief Mphofu and his family," Vin whispers in my ear.

Our friend Rose is the executive dean. She calls out the names of the graduating students, one by one, and they are each capped with a lot of cheering from the audience. When a blind student's name is read and he comes forward to be capped, everybody stands and people clap and cheer louder. People do not, in fact, sit down again or stop cheering and clapping until he is back in his seat. Even the dignitaries on the stage, the vice-chancellor and council, get on their feet and cheer.

In the evening we attend a dinner for senior officials of the university and its guests. Olga, the vice-chancellor's wife, has arrived from Pretoria, where she is dean of students at the University of South Africa. I'm glad to see her because she grew up in Mamelodi, where I grew up, and did graduate work at Harvard. Professor Nkondo introduces guests from outside the university, and when he comes to me, he introduces me as a respected political science professor from America. He also tells about meeting my father many years ago.

SATURDAY, MAY 8, 2004.
University of Venda, Thohoyandou.

Today is the second graduation day, and Vin and I are waiting in the lounge outside the vice-chancellor's office. She says it's important that I go inside and sit with the other distinguished guests, but I decline. I'm enjoying the conversations with some staff people.

We are served coffee, and before I finish my coffee, Professor Nkondo comes out and persuades me to join the keynote speaker and his wife and three members of the council in the inner lounge of his office. He then introduces us to one another. I'm glad to see his wife again, and as we chat, I remember Mamelodi.

I'm also glad when the wife of the guest speaker says she is from Moruleng and tells me her maiden name, a Setswana name. I tell her I know the name. When I also tell her I know Moruleng, she laughs and says, "Of course I know you know!"

The vice-chancellor has told the group he knew my father at Unisa and that my father was not only brilliant but also kind and humble. "I looked up to him with deep respect," he adds. I'm embarrassed when he turns to me and smiles and says, "And she is, of course, as you know, brilliant."

"Not quite," I say, and then one of the council members says, "You know it's true when they deny it."

As everybody laughs, I make a note to myself to ask Professor Nkondo one day when we are alone to please not say anything so nice about me when I'm there, because I get embarrassed.

I'm glad when all this is interrupted and we are led to the hall where the graduation will be held. Today we sit in the front row, and again everyone cheers as each student's name is called and they cross the stage to be capped. The last student to be called is the only PhD candidate who is graduating. He gets a standing ovation. He is from the Cameroon and is receiving a science degree.

The reception after the ceremony is pleasant, and I enjoy meeting everybody. I'm struck by how everyone knows at least one other person I know.

Back at the house that evening, Rose joins us and talks about how when she was working at Pretoria University she stopped going to meetings because they spoke Afrikaans. When the chair of the department said she had to attend meetings, she told him it was a waste of time because she didn't understand much . . . but she'd go if they spoke English. She says sometimes they'd start with English, but then quickly deteriorate into Afrikaans, at which point she'd just walk out. When the chair urged her to attend, she always said, "I can't sit in a meeting where I don't understand a word."

We also talk about how the University of Venda needs to get rid of certain departments that don't have students anymore, and Rose adds that Afrikaans is slated to go. Finally, we talk about how funding for black universities is inadequate.

SUNDAY, MAY 9, 2004.
Thohoyandou.

Kabelo calls this morning to say he needs a certified copy of the first page of my ID book. He also says he has faxed me, through Vin's office at the university, a form that will give him power of attorney for me. In the afternoon we go to Vin's office to take care of all this.

I also call our friend Irene's home. Her helper answers and says she's gone to Durban because her son, Shela, has been in a car accident and is apparently badly hurt. I immediately call Irene on her cell phone.

When she answers, she's crying. She tells me Shela is critical. His face is smashed and swollen, and he's on a ventilator. She says it was a car accident, and she was on her way to East London and about to board the plane at the airport when she received the call. Her daughter, Thando, is at the hospital with her. They will both be staying at Shela's place there in Durban.

I tell her we'll be praying for them, and that Shela is young and will recover. I also say I stand ready to come at a moment's notice if she needs me to. I talk to Thando and tell her, too, that it will work out and Shela will recover. Then I give the phone to Vin, and she also comforts Irene.

After we disconnect, Vin and I talk about how life can change in an instant. Finally, we fax the forms back to Kabelo and go home.

MONDAY, MAY 10, 2004.
Thohoyandou.

Vin and I call Irene and try to comfort her again. We also talk to Thando, who says she'll be at the hospital for a week. I tell her I can come to be with her mother when she leaves. When Irene says Shela is going to need a lot of reconstructive surgery, I tell her again that if she needs me to sit with her, I can come at a moment's notice.

Later I take a walk by myself to relieve my headache and stiff shoulders.

TUESDAY, MAY 11, 2004.
Thohoyandou.

Kabelo calls to tell me the meeting at the Land Commissioner's office went well. Uncle Gideon has not called back, but Kabelo heard from Tami that after checking the files, the Land Commission officer said Uncle Gideon had to share my grandmother Koko's house settlement with his siblings or, if they are deceased, with their children. Uncle Gideon had gone in earlier and asked the officer if he could take the whole amount from my grandmother's claim since he was her only surviving child. He had been hoping to get the whole amount. Kabelo also says he received a message from our brother that Uncle Gideon wants him to sign something. Kabelo says he'll call him tomorrow.

WEDNESDAY, MAY 12, 2004.
Thohoyandou.

Mbu and I talk about my proposal application for a grant to spend a year writing a novel about life in Kilnerton and the forced removals and their impact on the community. I want to write the story as fiction so I can make it more dramatic and bring it to life. I fill in the application form and he writes a letter of recommendation. He says he also wants to write about old Brakpan, where he grew up.

THURSDAY, MAY 13, 2004.
Thohoyandou.

When I call Kabelo, he says he spoke to Uncle Gideon, who wants him to come to his house in Mamelodi to sign an affidavit saying that we, our mother's children, have agreed not to be part of the beneficiaries on our mother's land claim.

"You see there are five of you for your parents' house and there are five of us here for Koko's house," he told him. Uncle Gideon wants me and my siblings to give up my mother's claim on my grandmother's Kilnerton house so he and my other uncles' children will get more money. This will mean my grandmother's money will be divided between her three sons and leave my mother, her daughter, out. Uncle Gideon thinks that since my siblings and I are getting money for our parents' house we should be satisfied with that.

Kabelo says he listened patiently and then told Uncle Gideon that this was a big issue. He also told him that he could not sign for all his siblings and that we would have a meeting and discuss this and then tell him what we've decided. Kabelo says he could sense the disappointment on our uncle's part.

Hearing my brother's report, I warn him not to be tricked into signing anything without consulting the rest of us. He assures me he will not.

"Today I'm going to meet with the officer who handles our claim to give him Dimake's children's birth certificates," he then tells me. "The officer has asked for them because they will get their father's share. This is the last document the officer needs to finalize our claim and authorize payment."

"Thank you for representing us," I tell him. "And for running around on our behalf."

THURSDAY, MAY 20, 2004.
Thohoyandou.

During my morning walk, I see a woman with a little stall at the corner of the main road. I greet her in Sepedi and she greets me back in Venda, the language of the area.

She smiles. "I understand Sepedi but do not speak it well," she says.

"It's the same for me with Venda," I say, smiling back. "I understand it but cannot speak it well."

When she asks me where I come from, I tell her and explain why I'm here.

"I hope you enjoy your stay," she tells me. She's crocheting a bag using strips cut from a black trash bag.

I gesture toward the bag. "How much do these bags cost?"

"Twenty rands," she says.

"How long does it take for you to make one?" I ask.

"If I work at it the whole day, say from eight to five, it takes two days," she says.

This means she makes ten dollars a day ($1.30 in 2004). This makes me sad, so I promise to come tomorrow and buy the one she's making now.

Her face lights up and she smiles. "Thank you, Auntie."

When I ask where she lives, she points to a hill in the distance and says she walks here every day and sells little things from her stall like gum, lollipops, and single cigarettes. She also has a public phone set up. But during the thirty-five minutes I spend at her stall, only two customers

come, a young man passing by on foot who buys one ciga-
rette and a man who stops to use the public phone.

While I'm still there, a car screeches to a stop just after
passing us, then backs up and stops next to the stall. A man
gets out and greets us. He shakes my hand and reminds
me that we met at the dinner after graduation the Saturday
before last.

"Would you like a ride back to your house?" he asks.

"Thank you but no," I say. "I'm taking a walk for exercise."

FRIDAY, MAY 21, 2004.
Thohoyandou.

We leave Vin's house in Thohoyandou, Venda for her main
house in Midrand at about six o'clock in the evening. Driving in the dark, we hit what we think was a little animal,
though we're not exactly sure what. We get out and check
but can't find anything besides a crack on the right front
headlight. I'm grateful it wasn't a big animal. I've heard
many stories about people being killed in collisions with big
animals crossing the road at night. I also think of stories of
people being attacked at night when they get out of their cars
to check for damage.

We arrive safely at Vin's house here in Midrand after
midnight.

SATURDAY, MAY 22, 2004.
Midrand to Johannesburg.

This morning, when Vin goes to Mamelodi, Mbu and I stay home reading newspapers. In the leading weekly paper there is an article by a well-known black academic about how the black principal of Wits University is said to not have a stellar academic background, and yet here he is, the new principal at the University of the North-West, formerly the white Afrikaner university with the unsavory reputation of having produced H.F. Verwoerd, the chief architect of apartheid. This new principal has been in higher education for only two years and is not an academic. But there is no outcry, and they say they chose him for his managerial expertise.

This reminds me of what my uncle Israel used to say—for whites, no black person is ever good enough in anything, so proving yourself to them is a waste of time and energy. The best course, he said, was to simply focus on doing our best.

Around six o'clock, we drive to an AIDS event in Windybrow at Newtown in Johannesburg. The Windybrow building used to be the home of a wealthy mining magnate, but now it is used as a theater. Mbu will be one of the speakers at tonight's event.

We arrive there early, and a young woman takes us inside to show us where we'll be seated in the front row. Then she takes us upstairs and says we can relax here and enjoy refreshments. After the event, we will gather with the other speakers and honored guests, have food and drinks, and mingle.

We are introduced to the other speakers. Most people know each other. Two well-known supreme court judges I know are there, and the writer Nadine Gordimer is also there. I'm glad to be in the company of people who fought in various ways in the struggle against apartheid. I also meet a white Zambian man who is friends with Nadine Gordimer. He tells me he is here in South Africa to get dental work done. When I tell him I went to the United States in 1978 to attend graduate school at Boston University, he smiles and says his son completed his graduate work at BU in 1978 and now lives in New York.

I also meet a woman from the Danish embassy. When she asks me if I've ever been to Denmark, I say I haven't been but hope to visit someday, maybe to give a talk at a university or something. We exchange cards and she asks how long I'll be visiting South Africa. She hopes we'll get a chance to get together at the embassy.

Around eight o'clock we are all ushered into the hall, which is filled with people. We take our seats and the proceedings begin. The emcee talks about the event, and then we listen to speeches by Gordimer, the two judges, and Mbu, all of them inspiring. Finally, a male gospel group performs. After the event, we retire to the hospitality room, where there is good food, good wine, and great conversations. It has been a most pleasant and inspiring evening.

I also meet an American professor who is here with a group of students. They're spending six weeks in Cape Town and six weeks in Johannesburg. I'm glad to hear his program is going well. I'm also glad to meet Justice C, who lived in the United States before the end of apartheid.

A few of us hang out until around two thirty in the morning, so it is four thirty by the time we get back to Vin's house in Midrand.

SUNDAY, MAY 23, 2004.
Midrand.

The story of the South African mercenaries caught in Zimbabwe continues in the newspapers. A white former South African Security officer who is now in prison here in South Africa is quoted as saying that one of the mercenaries in Zimbabwe was involved in the murder of an ANC official in Zimbabwe. Given this information, it should not come as a surprise that the South African government is not bending over backward to help the mercenaries.

Some people are arguing that South Africa should ask Zimbabwe to extradite the mercenaries so they can be tried here in South Africa. A South African government official has commented that there are hundreds of South Africans languishing in jails all over the world. They serve their sentences where they broke the law. I think that's how it should be; why should people who break the law of another country not be tried where they committed the crime and serve their sentences there? Furthermore, South Africa should not set a precedent in which they have to negotiate extradition for everyone.

MONDAY, MAY 24, 2004.
Midrand.

In a radio talk show this morning, a representative of the Landless People Movement complains that government officials are failing to help people who are being evicted from farms. He says that a representative of the Land Commission should refer these cases to his office.

Another caller says the mercenaries caught in Zimbabwe are the same people who murdered many anti-apartheid activists in Angola, Mozambique, and Namibia. He has no sympathy for them. They are the scum of the earth.

A government official says the government will wait for the judicial system to take its course. It is also said that the South African intelligence services tipped off the Zimbabwean government about the flight of the mercenaries from South Africa to Zimbabwe.

TUESDAY, MAY 25, 2004.
Midrand to Pretoria.

This morning I am on my way to meet Kabelo at the bank, where he is waiting for me with the documents. I need to open a new account because my previous account, which I have not used since 2001, has been closed. It is more difficult to open an account now because the government has issued new regulations requiring banks to verify the addresses of their clients. The only way I can prove that I live with my brother is to have him fill in a form and present electricity and water bills in his name for that address.

The young man who helps us checks our documents and says they are fine. It helps that our last names are the same. He helps us fill in all the forms, enters information in the computer, and opens my new account. I'm relieved.

Back at Vin's Midrand house, she is not feeling well, so we take her to the doctor, who orders a week's break from work. I don't mind spending this week here in Midrand and going back to Venda next week with Mbu and Vin. With them I am able to get a lot of work done without interruption and I am grateful for their invitation to go back and forth between their Midrand home and University of Venda, where Vin works as communications director.

MONDAY, MAY 31, 2004.
Midrand.

Vin was admitted to the hospital yesterday. She is dehydrated. This morning, Mbu and I drive to the offices of the Arts Council to submit my application for a research grant to be used for my Kilnerton book. On the way back, we pick up Vin at the hospital and bring her home. One of Vin's relatives is visiting us. She tells me about a phone conversation she had with a friend whose husband left the family when the children were still young and went to live with a woman with many children. She shakes her head. "He raised those children and neglected his own."

I tell her about my uncle, who also left his children and went to live with another woman. He improved that woman's house and later, when he was old and sick, the woman threw him out. Only then did he realize the house was in the woman's daughter's name only. Some of his children refused to take him back, but his youngest child took him to live with them. He died a year later.

When Vin's relative says she's going to remove the laundry from the drying line outside, I offer to go with her. While we are taking down the laundry, she informs me that people steal laundry from lines these days. Thieves stole laundry from her neighbor in broad daylight. They didn't steal everything, just the son's fashionable and expensive clothes. They scaled a high wall to get in. I say we have to be glad they did not enter the house and find the woman alone and harm her.

TUESDAY, JUNE 1, 2004.
Pretoria.

While I am waiting in town in Pretoria for a Mabopane taxi, a man approaches and shakes my hand, and asks if I remember him.

"I remember your face," I tell him, "but I forget your name."

"You are Lesego, and we met in Atlanta around 1981," he says. "I knew one of your brothers." Then he tells me his story and how he couldn't get a Foreign Service job because he was not an ANC member.

I nod in understanding. "Those jobs are usually political," I say. "They almost always go to the ANC members.

"They say they want people with foreign languages," he says. "I speak fluent French, but that did not help me."

The taxi arrives, so I say good-bye and get in the car. It quickly fills up and, as usual, we are overcrowded. Given the taxis' safety records, I am grateful when we reach Mabopane safely. I am happy to join Kabelo here at our parents' house, and look forward to spending a few days gardening and reading.

WEDNESDAY, JUNE 16, 2004.
Mabopane.

On this day, June 16, in 1976, thousands of students in Soweto marched peacefully to demonstrate against the apartheid government's Bantu Education policy in general and specifically against the apartheid government's mandate that the hated language of apartheid, Afrikaans, was to be used as a medium of instruction in African schools. This protest was the culmination of a long struggle and opposition to the government's Bantu Education policy, which was designed to deliberately provide inferior education to African students. The government at that time spent ten times more on white students than on black students. Education was free for white students, but not for African students.

The march was to end with a big rally at Orlando Stadium, but the heavily armed police fired tear gas and live ammunition at the unarmed, peacefully demonstrating students, killing many. The protest turned into a revolt that spread throughout the country, and images of black children massacred by the police quickly spread all over the world, galvanizing international opposition to apartheid.

This morning, thirty-eight years later, a caller on the radio program, a white woman, says she remembers June 16, 1976. She was sixteen years old and became anxious when she saw smoke over Soweto, but adults did not wish to talk about it. She couldn't believe people her age could do such a thing. She knew something was seriously wrong, and that was when she became politically conscious.

Another caller, a white teacher, says that white people who did not want to know about black suffering were suddenly forced to see what was happening—police and soldiers shooting unarmed black high school students who had what everybody in the world could recognize as legitimate grievances regarding the education policy for black people—that day.

The following day, June 17, 1976, riots exploded in Mamelodi, which is where I lived at the time. I tried to drive to my cousin's place in Mamelodi East, and as I approached the corner near Mamelodi High School, I realized that it was blocked; I turned around, parked in one of the side streets, and then walked to the corner to see what was happening. There was a large crowd and a boy lay on the ground, motionless. Nobody was helping him. A white soldier stood on an army tank a few feet away, pointing his gun at the boy on the ground. When two women tried to approach to help the boy, the white man on the tank shouted at them in Afrikaans to move back. "This is someone's child!" one of the women screamed, and she began to cry. We stood there, the crowd getting bigger and bigger, and for a long time the boy just lay there without help.

Later police vans came and the boy was thrown in the back of one of the vans. Later that day we found out who he was, and that he had died.

I was glad my younger brother was home when I got there. I told him what had happened and warned him not to go out. That night smoke went up in Mamelodi as government buildings, including the government liquor stores and administrative offices, were burned. We were worried about my brother, who broke his promise to stay home. We were all relieved when he returned around 10:00 p.m. When I asked him where he'd been, he said he'd gone all around town. He was the first to tell us that the municipal offices had been torched, along with the government-owned liquor stores.

My mother told him not to venture outside the following day, as the soldiers would be sure to shoot any black young man.

For the rest of that winter of 1976, the news reported disturbances all over the country almost every day.

SATURDAY, JUNE 19, 2004.
Mabopane.

During open question time at the neighborhood committee meeting today, speaker after speaker complains about services. The water was shut off for maintenance part of each day for three days last week, and residents were not informed ahead of time that this would happen. Another speaker says the councilor for the area refuses to attend meetings, and yet another complains about potholes in the streets. The acting police chief says he would like to work with the neighborhood association. A minister complains about theft at his church and people buying stolen property. He says people should not buy stolen property because, "If they can steal from somebody else, they will steal from you one day." There are also complaints about empty stands in the neighborhood. At the end of the meeting we listen to music and have drinks donated by the neighborhood store.

SUNDAY, JUNE 20, 2004.
Mabopane.

Two of Kabelo's friends, Martha and Lily, are frequent visitors. When they come to visit today, Martha brings a dress that she wishes to have altered. Kabelo agrees to do it while they wait. I sit with them and enjoy their stories, always hoping there'll be more of them. I'm not disappointed, as Martha launches into a new topic: how theft is rampant in the area and thieves break in at night while people are sleeping and rob them.

"In the next street over," she says, "thieves broke in at night, tied the people up, then loaded televisions and other electronic gadgets and stole both cars."

"I've heard that the night thieves use a magic doll," Lily says. "It's an ordinary-looking doll like the little girls play with, except it's one that has been worked with secret medicine and magic."

"How do the thieves use it, exactly?" I ask.

"They throw it against the door," she explains. "It sticks and the locked door miraculously opens."

Having learned not to ruin a good story with questions that require scientific explanations, I just smile and say, "The thieves must move around very quietly."

"Yes," Martha says, "they use embalming fluid." Before I can ask how they use it, she says, "They just sprinkle it around the house and in the yard, and it puts everybody inside the house into deep sleep."

I smile. "It's dangerous magic."

Kabelo winks at me and smiles.

As is often the case these days, the conversation ends up veering toward the impact of AIDS. Lily tells me of many cases of AIDS deaths in the neighborhood and how they have to attend funerals most weekends. They talk about a woman they all know who is infected and now sleeps with many men, and sometimes even boys, to infect them. Martha talks about two young lovers in the neighborhood who died within a week of each other. What made it even sadder is that the families now don't speak to each other because each blames the other's child for having infected their child.

Then the conversation switches to America.

"What does it feel like to live there?" Lily asks.

I give my standard reply—that I like it a lot and am happy there. "But life is life," I add, "and it has its own challenges, wherever you are." I tell them about a Buddhist writer who said, "Wherever you go, there you are."

"Auntie, we always say how you are not like other people who have lived in America," Martha says.

This is, of course, not the first time someone has said that to me on this trip, but I'm always curious about their reasons. I ask her to explain what she means.

She says I speak normally, with no affectation, and I dress nicely but not in a flashy way. She points to my skirt, which is made of *motoishi*, a popular cotton print material that most black women use. "You even wear ordinary *motoishi* like us," she says.

"You see?" she says to Lily. "I told you Auntie will not change. She remains nice and respectful of others, even if they are ordinary."

Hearing that, I laugh and say I'm home; I'm not going to work or some special event, so why would I dress like I'm going to work or somewhere formal? Besides, there are elegant *motoisha* materials that are sewn in fancy patterns and are suitable for more formal festive occasions.

"No, Auntie," Martha says. "You don't understand. You are not a show-off. You talk with us nicely. You also speak pure Setswana, not mixing in English like the other people do who are trying to impress, and they are not even as educated."

All I can say is, "We are all special, in different ways."

Martha shakes her head. Then she asks me another question: "How much do the American flag blankets cost?"

She and Lily are both surprised when I say I've never seen one. I ask her to describe it. The description she gives me doesn't help much.

"Did you see it in a picture somewhere, or maybe in a magazine?" I ask.

"No," she says, "one of my aunt's friends had one, but she was not forthcoming about where she got it."

"Has your aunt's friend ever been to America?" I ask.

She laughs. "No," she says in a loud voice. "But I am prepared to save all my money if you can get one for me in America."

I don't promise anything; I do suggest, however, that since her aunt's friend has never been to America, she probably got the flag blanket at one of the stores in Johannesburg that import things from China. "It might be helpful to look in those stores," I tell her.

Kabelo has completed the alteration by now, so Martha and Lily leave. I tell Kabelo I wish he would write down all these fantastic stories he hears when I'm not around. He laughs and says he'd never find time to do his work if he did that. I wish I had time to sit with him every day while he sews and listens to his customers' conversations. He says he purposely suggested that Martha and Lily wait while he did their alterations because he knew I would enjoy their stories.

As I thank him and get up to go back inside the house, a young man named Peter comes to pick up pants Kabelo has repaired. He sits down and asks if we've heard about the death of a girl a few streets down. Kabelo tells him he heard and says it is sad that young people are dying. Peter tells Kabelo she got a disease from an older man.

"Girls these days are so materialistic," he laments. "They go with older working men for money."

"Boys are just as materialistic," Kabelo says. "And since they can't go with older lovers, they steal and rob."

Peter chuckles. "You're right, Uncle. Everybody wants easy money these days. They don't like to work hard."

I bid them both good-bye and go back inside the house.

I read an article on page 7 of the *City Press* about eighty-one-year-old Martha Mahlangu, the mother of struggle hero Solomon Mahlangu, who was executed by the government on April 6, 1979. They lived in Mamelodi, the township where I lived until I came to the United States. My uncle Gideon was a close friend of the family.

The article quotes Martha: "I can't read. I can't write—but everything is in my heart. Everything that happened. Yes, everything that I know."

Solomon never fired a single shot. When his mother was told her son was going to be executed, she said, "We know that we must all die, but if they come and tell you on Monday that they are going to kill your child on Friday, how are you going to feel during the long week?" She answered her own question. "Are you going to eat? Drink? Or sleep? What are you going to do? Oh, it was a terrible day, you couldn't believe it. And Solomon killed nobody."

A few years later, during the state of emergency in the 1980s and several years after Solomon's execution, the security police arrested his mother and kept her in jail without charge. "I was in jail for the whole year," she said. "The first week I was in Gezina [the police station]. Without anything to eat or to drink. Alone."

I make a mental note to ask Uncle Gideon to introduce me to Martha Mahlangu and help me persuade her to let me help her tell her story in a full biography. She still lives in Mamelodi, and it would be easy for me to stay with my uncle for a while and go to interview her every day.

It has always been my intention to help tell the stories of the people who loved our heroes. That is what drove me to write the novel I've just completed, *Matters of Life and Death*, which is about the family of a young man (not Solomon Mahlangu) who is sentenced to Robben Island.

At the entrance to Mamelodi there is a big statue of Solomon. I make a mental note to spend some time there again, and to visit Solomon's mother, next time I go to Mamelodi.

SATURDAY, JUNE 26, 2004.
Mabopane.

The city councilor for our ward has called a meeting for today at Matshidiso Primary School, which is around the corner from the house. I arrive at the venue just after 11:00 a.m. and see an ANC activist I know, a young man named Simon. When I ask him why he's going in the opposite direction, he informs me he's running home to make a telephone call to the councilor's office because he's not there. I go in and they pass around a paper for everybody to write their names and addresses.

Some officials—but not the councilor—arrive at the meeting, which begins around eleven forty-five. The chairman opens the meeting by announcing that the officials will make brief remarks, and then there will be ample time for questions and answers. As the official from the Water Affairs Department talks about how they're making improvements, a man in front interrupts him.

"Why did you not tell us you were shutting water down the other day?" he asks.

Before the official can reply, another man jumps up and asks, "Why does so much water get wasted?"

The emcee stands up at this point and says there should be one question at a time and people should wait their turns. The official, instead of answering these questions, merely says people should call the Water Department if there are any problems.

Another man stands up. "I called the department on

three occasions and reported problems, but nothing has been done for a long time," he says.

I wish Kabelo were here to explain to me how water is wasted and to interpret other things for me.

The official next says that water rates will go up, but he doesn't know by how much. Notices will go out soon with all relevant information.

There is groaning throughout the room, and a woman stands up and says, "We are not pleased with the councilor not showing up. We deserve more respect from someone who is supposed to serve the community." The emcee says he has not been provided with any information about the councilor's plans and hopes he's on his way.

The official from the Environment and Tourism Affairs Department stands up next and says all wards are being asked by the Metro Council to name the streets, and all streets should hold meetings to decide on street names. (As in most black townships, there are only house numbers and no street names in this area.) When a woman asks why the streets are not repaired, the river area is not cleaned, and the grass is not cut, the emcee points out that these are some of the issues the councilor should come and address.

When the woman from the Social Development Department says she has to talk about food parcels now so she can run to a conference in Pretoria, the chairman says it's not on the agenda and can be postponed.

Another man stands up. "What about these workmen at the park?" he demands. "They sit under the trees doing nothing most of the time."

"Yes, this is a problem," the Environment Department official agrees. "There needs to be more supervision." He suggests that the community take responsibility for open areas and that people will be arrested if they do anything illegal at the park.

"The council should be more responsive to the community," a man says.

"There is no follow-through, only promises," another complains.

Another man complains about streetlights that don't work, and an obviously frustrated man shouts, "We need a speed bump on our street! These cars go so fast, it's only a matter of time before our children are killed."

Finally, around 1:15 p.m., a man walks into the hall. I can tell from people's reactions that this is the councilor. But I have doubts about him. He looks unsteady and has bloodshot eyes. Is he drunk?

A man who has been one of the most vocal at the meeting stands up and struts out, clucking his tongue loudly as he passes the table where the officials are sitting. More people follow him, walking out in protest. I join them. Everybody except the officials ends up walking out.

Outside the hall, Mrs. Mashiane invites me to visit the community garden with her. She drives us there, and on the way we talk about how it's a pity the councilor behaves this way. They hope he won't be on the ANC list next time.

Mrs. Mashiane shows me around the community gardens. I congratulate her for having created something so big and so useful to the community. In 1995, she approached town officials with a proposal to use the vacant land for community gardens. She reminded them there was a lot of poverty and unemployment, and people could learn to garden and feed their families. The gardens that she and her husband and son have built here have lots of vegetables, including spinach, mustard greens, string beans, and cabbage.

"I thought about taking them to the wholesale market

this week, but prices are not good," she says. "We will take the produce next week and see what happens."

As we continue walking around the gardens, I'm surprised to see strawberries.

"I try to plant a variety of plants that are not common in local gardens," Mrs. Mashiane says.

"How many people tend the garden?" I ask.

"At the beginning, I had one hundred five people working in the gardens, but the number is much smaller now," she says. "Given the high unemployment rate, I am surprised and disappointed that more people are not prepared to come to work in the gardens."

"What kind of people do come?" I ask.

"It's mostly women," she says. "Many of them are grandmothers trying to feed their grandchildren."

I buy a lot of vegetables. When Mrs. Mashiane's husband arrives, we talk and look around for a while longer before I leave to go home.

Back at home, I find two women who were at the councilor's meeting. I tell them the meeting was a practical education for me, and Kabelo laughs and says the women have told him the whole story.

SUNDAY, JUNE 27, 2004.

Mabopane.

I get up early today, excited that my friend Snowy will be arriving from Johannesburg around 9:00 a.m. to spend the whole day with me. We grew up together in Mamelodi, and I remember how we studied together for final exams—she for her final year of high school exams and I for my college exams. She lived one street over from me, and for three weeks, she came to my house every day so we could study together.

It feels good to know that I will spend the day with someone I've known since childhood. Snowy married a man who comes from Thaba Nchu, where I went to boarding school for my first three years of high school. She is one of the people I always looked forward to seeing when I came home for school holidays. She's told me she's bringing a friend today, someone she knows I'll like. I'm looking forward to meeting the friend.

I cook spinach, cabbage, fennel, potatoes, and chicken before they arrive so I don't have to do more cooking when Snowy and her friend are here.

Snowy arrives and gives me a big bouquet of flowers with carnations and roses. Then she turns to her friend and says, "Vera, this is my sister."

I hug Vera, who smiles and says, "I've heard so many good things about you, I didn't believe someone like you actually existed."

"I've always thought of Snowy as my younger sister," I tell her. I turn to Snowy. "These flowers are beautiful!"

Snowy turns to Vera and says, "I must have told you this. Mummy, her mother, had a prize-winning vegetable and flower garden. These flowers are nothing. Hers were spectacular. People would stop to look at the garden. I don't know how she did it while teaching. She was amazing."

"Yes, you told me about the beautiful flowers many times," Vera says. "You said you promised yourself a garden as beautiful as that when you grew up."

Snowy laughs. "Mine isn't too bad, but it doesn't come close."

"Your garden is lovely, but it cannot compete with a memory," I say.

"I'm so happy to finally meet you," Vera says.

Now Snowy tells me Vera was the first volunteer for home-based AIDS health care. Vera says AIDS has devastated families. There are families now headed by seventeen-year-olds, even fifteen-year-olds, who depend on the generosity of neighbors and churches and nongovernmental organizations (NGOs). The luckier AIDS orphans are being raised by their grandparents, who themselves depend on meager government social grants. Vera adds she worked for nine years as a volunteer, but now she's burnt out and is taking a break. But since she pioneered the home-based model, she is often called upon to train community workers all over the country, which she still enjoys.

We spend the afternoon together catching up. It is a memorable day. Before they leave, they go to Kabelo, who is sewing in the garage, and bid him good-bye. He apologizes for not spending time with them, and explains that it's because he's been so busy making clothes for a weekend event.

They drive off, and I go back in the house and pick up the glasses we drank from in the living room. I find a red package on a side table. When I open it, I find a beautiful multicolor bead necklace made with small, delicate beads. I scream, "Snowy!" and run out to Kabelo to show him and read him the note—"For you, my sister, I'm blessed." I also tell him about the beautiful flowers.

Kabelo touches the necklace. "This is a very high-end necklace," he says. "It has a special design."

I've never seen one like this. The beads are expensive and delicate. I am touched. I tell Kabelo I'm not going to call Snowy and merely thank her on the phone; instead, I am going to sit at my desk right away and write her the longest thank-you letter she has ever seen. First thing tomorrow morning, I will go to the post office and mail it express.

MONDAY, JUNE 28, 2004.
Mabopane.

When I get up and join Kabelo for breakfast in the kitchen, he tells me one of our neighbors came earlier to tell him that a young woman they know—she was about twenty-two years old and lived two streets away—has died, but they're not sure what from. She just collapsed and frothed in the mouth and died before they could get her to the hospital.

"She was very overweight," Kabelo says. "She was so big, she had difficulty walking. She did not look healthy for someone so young."

"Children are heavier these days," I say.

"The schools no longer teach physical education, and sports are no longer emphasized," he says, shaking his head.

After a few hours of reading inside the house, I come back out to the garage to join Kabelo and find two women, Rose and Mapula, sitting with him. Kabelo is used to keeping his head down and sewing on the machine while his customers and guests sit and talk. They are used to his quietness. But he hears everything, and in the evenings he tells me the stories he's heard. Some of them are strange. In periods of anxiety, rumors and myths abound.

Mapula says her sister, who works in a government mortuary in Middelburg, which is five hours away, visited her last weekend and told her about some of the things that happen at her job. Her sister said they keep two guns on the table at work.

"What makes the mortuary so dangerous that they need guns?" I ask.

Mapula laughs. "They are not afraid of people coming from the outside to harm them," she says. "There's no money at the mortuary. It's that sometimes people die and come back, and once in a while someone wakes up at the mortuary, and the workers just shoot them because it is too much of a headache to deal with them."

"That seems unkind," I say.

She says these people who die and come back may cause problems if allowed to rejoin society. They may come back from the land of the dead with strange powers and cause problems.

I remember not to argue so as to keep the stories going. Kabelo often points out that arguing is a waste of energy sometimes.

After they leave, Kabelo says the sister who works at the morgue was probably just entertaining Mapula with her stories.

TUESDAY, AUGUST 3, 2004.
Mabopane.

When the taxi driver looks at my grocery bags and jokes, "Looks like you have good food. And meat," I laugh and say, "Meat? Who can afford it? It's so expensive these days."

Then everybody in the taxi laughs, and a woman says, "Who can afford it? It is chicken feet for us these days."

"Meat is for Sundays only," another one says.

"Every Sunday?" the driver asks.

"No," says the woman. "One Sunday a month."

We laugh again, and I regret that I'm the first one to get out. As I gather my things, one of the women says, "Chicken is too expensive these days, too," and a man says, "And it tastes awful these days."

"They sell us chicken from other countries," a young man says. "That's why it's expensive and tastes bad. I don't even think it is chicken. That's not real chicken. Have you ever seen a chicken with such huge thighs?"

"It is the hormones they feed them," I say, "and God knows what else." I get out of the taxi and close the door. The driver smiles and waves at me as he pulls away. I gather my bags and walk home.

On the radio a woman relates how she made a call to an agent in Cape Town about accommodation in London, where she planned to go on vacation. When she arrived in

Heathrow Airport in England, she called the hostel. The woman who answered the phone asked her if she was black, and when she said yes, the woman told her they only take white people, and before she could respond, the woman hung up. The hostel, which is owned by South Africans, is apparently well known.

The radio host says he is surprised they could be that blatant, but then again, he is not surprised. The caller adds that she too was not surprised—inconvenienced, but not surprised. Other people call in to express disapproval of the hostel owner's response.

There is also a report about New York being on high terrorism alert. I miss the United States, especially Boston. It feels strange to be homesick for my adopted home in the United States while I'm in South Africa, the home of my birth.

"Do you remember the Fikile family in Mamelodi?" Kabelo asks me this afternoon.

Of course I do. Their eldest son, Simon, used to be friends with our older brothers.

"Simon and his wife still live in their parents' house," Kabelo says. "They noticed that their coal supplies were running down too fast. They suspected someone must be raiding the coal drum behind the house."

"What did they do?" I ask, intrigued.

"This went on for some time," Kabelo says, "until Simon decided to do something about it. He told the neighbors about the problem, and they all expressed their sympathy. They were also angry, and lamenting that things have changed in Mamelodi. Thefts have increased. So Simon promised to sleuth around and get to the bottom of things."

One day, Kabelo explains, Simon asked his wife to

sweep around the coal drum so they would maybe see the direction of the footsteps. The theft happened several times a month, but on no fixed schedule. Several times, Simon sat in the dark by the kitchen window, but the thief did not come on those nights. One night, when he had not stayed up waiting to catch the thief, he noticed footsteps coming over the neighbor's fence. Trusting his neighbor and the other occupants of the house, Simon thought the coal thief had simply come through that yard and over the fence into Simon's yard.

One day he got lucky. He saw the thief open the coal drum. He rushed out as quietly as he could, ran around the house, and caught the thief bent over the drum. He hit him on the head and back.

"Uncle, please don't kill me, don't kill me!" the thief screamed. It was a voice Simon recognized. He tried to pull the thief up, but he was limp. Simon could not get him up. The thief lay there, collapsed on the ground. Simon was shocked when he saw who it was: the son of his trusted next-door neighbor.

"Sammy," he shouted, "look what you've done! Look what you've done!"

Sammy was crying, and when Simon tried to help him up, he could not move. They took the boy to the hospital, where he spent a long time. It turned out that he was paralyzed from the waist down. He had to get around in a wheelchair.

"I feel sorry for the boy but I also feel sorry for Simon," I say. "I'm sure he wanted to punish the thief but not to paralyze him."

"Everybody was surprised," Kabelo says. "Sammy wasn't known to be a troublemaker. Besides, his family had long ago given up their coal stove, so Sammy must have been stealing the coal to give to someone else."

I ask about the fallout in the community. Kabelo says

there is so much stealing these days that the people in the community supported Simon.

"When the police don't solve crimes, people get tired and take things into their own hands," I say. "Then they are cheered and seen as heroes, especially by those who have been victimized."

Kabelo agrees with me and reminds me of an incident in Mabopane a few years back: Someone was terrorizing the neighborhood by stealing tires from cars, even when those cars were parked in yards. The tire thief kept on stealing from one man in particular, Mr. Tsebe.

One day, Mr. Tsebe got a tip about who was taking his tires. The boy was a known thief, and Mr. Tsebe went to tell his parents to warn him. But the parents were rude; they swore at him and said the boy would not do such a thing.

A few nights later, Mr. Tsebe caught the boy stripping his car in the dark. He tied the boy up, put him in his car, and drove to the mountain beyond the township, where he burned him to death with a tire.

When the police investigated this crime, Mr. Tsebe was a suspect, but he denied any involvement. Many people supported Mr. Tsebe and were prepared to contribute cash toward his defense, should he be prosecuted. The case was never solved. Rumor had it that the boy had had so many brushes with the law—he had even stolen from a police officer's home—that the police did not apply themselves to solving his murder.

"How do they know Mr. Tsebe did it when it has not been proven?" I ask.

Kabelo shrugs. "No one can know for sure. It is possible that someone like him, who was tired of being victimized by these thefts, did it."

"That's how societies break down," I say.

MONDAY, AUGUST 9, 2004.
Mabopane.

Today is Women's Day, an official holiday commemorating the events of this day in 1956 when twenty thousand women from all over the country marched to the Union Buildings (the seat of the apartheid government in Pretoria) to protest the pass laws that restricted their freedom. The four leaders of the protest dumped the petitions—which had more than one hundred thousand signatures—at the door of Prime Minister J.G. Strydom's office. At the suggestion of Lilian Ngoyi, one of the protest's leaders, the women stood silently for thirty minutes and then broke into song as they dispersed, chanting, "*Wathin'Abafazi, Wathint'imbokodo.*" ("You have touched the women, you've struck a rock.")

One of today's newspapers refers to an international study showing that South Africa is among the top ten countries in the world in terms of women in government, with twelve women among twenty-eight cabinet ministers, ten among twenty-one deputy ministers, and four among nine provincial premiers. But even so, South Africa has a high rate of rape and abuse of women.

SUNDAY, AUGUST 15, 2004.
Mabopane.

The news in the papers today is about members of parliament and corruption in the travel voucher scandal and how the special investigative unit, the Scorpions, is investigating the members of parliament named as corrupt.

FRIDAY, AUGUST 20, 2004.
Pretoria.

I don't wish to start anything until nine thirty, when Kabelo will call the Land Affairs Office in town to find out if we have to go in. Shortly after nine thirty, I hear Kabelo shouting, "Money, money, checks."

"Let's go now," I say, and we take a taxi into town and go to the Land Affairs Office, where we wait. As we wait, a young man is called into the payout office. He's gone for a while, and the man sitting next to us says they are slow and incompetent. He tells us how they messed up his opportunity to buy a good farm from a white farmer and laments the incompetence and slowness of civil servants, for whom he has nothing but contempt.

After twenty minutes, the young man comes out of the office and the next person goes in.

Finally it is our turn. We go in. The young woman is courteous and polite, but slow. At the next desk over, two young men are visiting a young African woman. The three of them are talking and making noise the whole time. We sign some forms, and the young woman gives us each a voucher for R22,000 and directs us to the Absa Bank around the corner, where a check will be issued.

We are surprised when we get to the bank: we don't have to stand in line. Instead, we are directed to an office, where we sit comfortably as we are helped.

The young woman there smiles and says, "We've been processing a lot of these this week. Congratulations."

We go home feeling a mix of emotions—happy to finally receive this money, but also sad that our parents did not live to see this day and enjoy the compensation.

SATURDAY, AUGUST 21, 2004.
Mabopane.

This morning, Kabelo and I visit our parents' graves at the cemetery, which is not far away. We sit quietly for a while at the gravesite. Kabelo asks if I wish to talk, and I say he should talk, as he is the one who represented us in the long dealings with the Land Affairs Department. Besides, he's the one who came back home to live with our parents in their final years.

Kabelo inclines his head and begins speaking, thanking them for all they did for us and telling them he wishes they had lived to see this day.

The only thing I add is to promise that I will write the story of our family's lives in Kilnerton, and what it was like to have our land taken away. My journey through my home country is done. What's left for me is to begin writing.

SUNDAY, AUGUST 29, 2004.
Mamelodi.

Mbu calls around noon and says, "Congratulations!"

"For what?" I ask.

"I received a call that you got the research grant from the Arts Council," he says. "A letter to you is on its way."

All I can do at first is scream. Then I say, "Thank you, thank you for your help, Mbu. Your recommendation did it."

"No," he says. "Your proposal did it."

We resolve to celebrate with Vin the following day.

The remainder of my time at home will be devoted to doing research for my Kilnerton book and writing about this visit to my country of birth.

The best news? My American publisher has informed me that my novel, *Matters of Life and Death,* has a publication date of June 15 and I am invited to sign copies at their booth at Book Expo America in New York in May 2005.

My next travels in South Africa will be to the Northern Cape, the Northwest Province, and Gauteng, three areas where my people, Batswana, lived in My Father's Country.

WEDNESDAY, MAY 18, 2005.
Mamelodi and Johannesburg.

I have spent eleven months with Kabelo, and my travels are now done. I'm grateful for the R20,000 research grant I received from the National Arts and Culture Council to do research for my book—a story about Kilnerton as it was before it was destroyed by the apartheid government in 1954. I have spent these past months researching and writing about Kilnerton. It has been cathartic and I feel I can now move on.

Finally, the day of my departure is here and I'm ready to go back to Boston. I'm excited and looking forward to the publication of my first novel, *Matters of Life and Death*, by Genesis Press in the United States. I can't wait for May 5 launch at Book Expo America in New York.

Kabelo cooks a big dinner that includes lamb, which we eat at midday. I tell him how happy I am that we've had the opportunity to spend all this time together. I remember how happy our childhood was, and how close we always were. Our much older brothers went to boarding school when we were young, but since Kabelo and I were born about eighteen months apart, we grew up together.

"And we are lucky to have been brought up by Kokwana," Kabelo adds.

Kokwana took care of us. She moved from my grandmother's house, where she had lived for many years as a member of the family, to live with us when I was born.

"Yes, we were lucky to be raised by someone who loved us so much," I say.

"It was a blessing that our mother worked," Kabelo says, "and Kokwana, who was not nearly as strict, looked after us."

I laugh and agree, though I add, "Mother was very patient, too."

A few minutes later, Kabelo says it is going to be strange to adjust to my absence again. I assure him it won't be long before I'll be back; I'm coming next year for a couple of weeks to work with our lawyer to complete the settling of our father's estate. Kabelo promises to make me some new garments that I'm sure to like.

Our young neighbor, Cyril, who is taking me to the airport, arrives now, and we load my stuff into his car. As Kabelo and I hug, I assure him that we'll be seeing each other soon, so we don't have to be sad about parting. But I'm fighting tears, and his eyes are glistening too. I promise to call more often.

He's standing at the gate as we drive off, and we wave at each other until the car turns the corner.

"Why doesn't Kabelo come to the airport with us?" Cyril asks.

"He prefers to say his good-byes at home," I explain.

"He looks sad," Cyril says.

"It's all right," I reply. "I'll be back here before the end of next year."

At the airport in Johannesburg, Cyril waits for me while I check in. After I get my boarding pass, I hug him and thank him for a smooth trip.

Cyril begins to walk away, then stops. "Auntie, Uncle Kabelo is going to be all right," he says. "He always has people coming and going. When I go back, I'm going to sit with him while he sews as usual. I'll also bring him some

Oros, his favorite orange drink. And I'm going to make sure I'm the one picking you up when you come back next year."

All I can do is smile.

THURSDAY, MAY 19, 2005.
Boston.

The flight to Boston through Frankfurt was uneventful, and I am glad to be back in Boston. This is the first time I've entered the United States as a citizen, a fact that makes me smile as I stand in the line reserved for citizens. When I get outside, I'm greeted by a bright blue sky and crisp spring air.

I am happy to be in Boston, my new country. I am especially happy knowing that I will soon go back to visit South Africa, the country of my birth, once again.

ACKNOWLEDGMENTS

Thank you for your support and friendship: Brenda Randolph, Kitty Burke and TLC, Marian Saunders, Beryl Kalisa, Kamanzi Kalisa, Mary Ann Cloherty, Joanne Cavartota, Gene Cavartota, Anna Moshier, Cheryl Smith, Barbara Brown, Nancy Lane, Ellen Bambo, Rhoda Moyo, Becky Richardson, Jo Sullivan, Jeanne Wilson, Barbara Ardinger, Abigail McGrath, Linda Khoza, Anna Khabo, Kelesitse Mokae, Janet McGrath, Linda Sedibe, Mathabo Malepe, Shole Shole, Sekepe Matjila, George Lenyai, Nolanga Phetla, Krissa Lagos, Andre Howe, Cheryl Smith, and Yvonne Mogadime.

ABOUT THE AUTHOR

LESEGO MALEPE left apartheid South Africa with a Fulbright scholarship to study in the US in 1978. After completing her graduate work in political science at Boston University, she taught political science at a college near Boston for many years. She is the author of the novel *Matters of Life and Death*, published in 2005, about the family of a high school student who was sentenced to life on Robben Island in 1963. She has also contributed op-ed articles to national newspapers, including *USA Today*, the *Baltimore Sun*, the *San Francisco Chronicle*, and the *St. Louis Post Dispatch*. Malepe has served for many years as a judge for the Children's Africana Book Awards of the Outreach Council of the African Studies Association, and leads workshops for teachers about how to teach about Africa in general and how to use African literature in the classroom.

Author photo © Betsy Cullen

SELECTED TITLES FROM SHE WRITES PRESS

She Writes Press is an independent publishing company
founded to serve women writers everywhere.
Visit us at www.shewritespress.com.

The Beauty of What Remains: Family Lost, Family Found by
Susan Johnson Hadler. $16.95, 978-1-63152-007-5. Susan Johnson Hadler goes on a quest to find out who the missing people in
her family were—and what happened to them—and succeeds in
reuniting a family shattered for four generations.

Gap Year Girl by Marianne Bohr. $16.95, 978-1-63152-820-0.
Thirty-plus years after first backpacking through Europe, Marianne
Bohr and her husband leave their lives behind and take off on a year-
long quest for adventure.

*Godmother: An Unexpected Journey, Perfect Timing, and Small
Miracles* by Odile Atthalin. $16.95, 978-1-63152-172-0. After thirty
years of traveling the world, Odile Atthalin—a French intellectual
from a well-to-do family in Paris—ends up in Berkeley, CA, where
synchronicities abound and ultimately give her everything she has
been looking for, including the gift of becoming a godmother.

Loveyoubye: Holding Fast, Letting Go, And Then There's The Dog
by Rossandra White. $16.95, 978-1-938314-50-6. A soul-searching
memoir detailing the painful, but ultimately liberating, disintegra-
tion of a twenty-five-year marriage.

*Don't Call Me Mother: A Daughter's Journey from Abandonment to
Forgiveness* by Linda Joy Myers. $16.95, 978-1-938314-02 -5. Linda
Joy Myers's story of how she transcended the prisons of her childhood
by seeking—and offering—forgiveness for her family's sins.

This is Mexico: Tales of Culture and Other Complications by Carol
M. Merchasin. $16.95, 978-1-63152-962-7. Merchasin chronicles
her attempts to understand Mexico, her adopted country, through
improbable situations and small moments that keep the reader
moving between laughter and tears.